D1189852

LEGAL THINGS PARENTS SHOULD KNOW

With Occasional **Wit** and **Sarcasm**

CINDY K. CAMPBELL

DISCLAIMER

Everything stated in this book is for informational purposes only and not for the purpose of providing legal advice. The use of the information contained herein does not create an attorney-client relationship between the reader and the author. You should contact an attorney to obtain advice with respect to any particular issue or problem you are experiencing and your attorney will be able to advise you on the best way to proceed.

Printed in the United States of America.

Interior design by FormattedBooks

CONTENTS

ABOUT ME

In case you are wondering who I am and why you should give a care about the things I'm saying, I will fill you in a little about my life.

I am an attorney who focuses on estate planning and collaborative divorce/mediation. I am the proud partner of a firm named Campbell Long based out of Chicago, Illinois. Campbell Long is owned and operated by women—actually, by moms—who all seek to help families through their legal problems in an approachable way. The firm offers services on estate planning (wills and trusts), administration (helping the family after a loved one passes), guardianship (becoming the caregiver over a child or disabled adult), and collaborative divorce and mediation (a "friendlier" way to split).

How I got here

One of the first law firms I ever worked for was a small estate-planning firm in Mission Viejo, California. I quickly learned I loved doing transactional law (meaning contracts, wills, business documents, etc). I loved it so much that I worked there from my second year in law school until I graduated. I went on to basically have my own satellite office in Newport Beach, California, right on the bay. I mean, *hell yeah!* I felt on top of the world, working with amazing clients at a small boutique firm, specializing in helping people with estate planning and small business stuff. I was in a wonderful location, which coincidentally was down the street from my house, and I felt like my life was pretty much all rainbows.

Then, I graduated in the *awesome* year of 2008. Remember that year? Yeah, that year when we had a little housing market crash which ended up causing the great recession? No one, and I mean *no* one was handing out legal jobs at that point. I wasn't particularly worried, though, because I already had my dream job all lined up. You know, the one basket where I put all my eggs, betting on it all working out.

Of course, you guessed it: that dream job was soon swiftly taken away. People were now losing their estates and not so worried about spending money to protect them. It was one of those moments that changed the path of my life—and however hard it was at the time, I now realize I'm grateful for it. I looked high and low for a job, but a job for a law student who only had estate planning experience, was not out there. So, I started looking for any job—I mean, *ANY* job! Dog walker? Sales associate at a pet shop? (Yes, I'm an animal lover if you can't tell by now.)

At one point, I was being interviewed for that associate sales position at the local pet store and the woman said to me, "You just graduated from law school?"

I said, "Yes, that is correct, but I will work really hard and I'm a very good sales person."

She looked at me again and said, "I think you're overqualified for this position."

Yeah, *no shit,* lady! I went on to tell her how much I loved animals and how hard of a worker I was, but needless to say, I didn't get the job.

So, I went back to my law school and spoke with the career counselor. She asked what other areas of law I was interested in. I told her about a mediation class I really enjoyed, and she recommended I reach out to the professor who taught the class and see if she had any recommendations for me. Thankfully, she did!

She told me to go volunteer and get certified in mediation. Though it was not what I wanted to hear (as my student debt was practically doubling by the day), it was something. So, I reached out to the Orange County Human Relations Commission and started volunteering at various courthouses. After many hours of volunteering, I got certified in basic and advanced mediation.

Oh, and in the meantime, because God laughs when you're making plans, I took and did *not* pass the California bar (notably the hardest bar exam, especially at that time) by missing 3.5 multiple choice questions. So I was let go from my dream job, I had student debt in the $200k-plus range (and literally growing by the minute), I was *volunteering* to keep my resume up to date, and I had just been notified that I did not pass the flipping test to get licensed for a job I didn't have and that wasn't around, anyway!

Luckily, I find that when the world throws you out into the ocean and you are just about to sink, it tends to throw you a life vest. I was nearly drowning, but I soon started realizing that I really loved mediation and solving disputes amicably. I always wanted to help people in my career, and felt so strongly about using my legal knowledge—combined with the patience and ability to remain objective—to help settle people's disputes. Also, through volunteering so much and getting my 120-hour Advanced Mediation Certification (and then going on for the Advanced Family Mediation Certification), I found myself to be quite good at it. I just kind of "got it," if you know what I mean.

You know when sometimes you want something so bad and you keep trying and trying and then all of a sudden, this other thing that just lands in your lap and works out so easily? I suppose that is what they call *natural talent*. I stepped into this new role and immediately felt like I could do this and make a difference. Also, I had a really good settlement percentage and almost none of my mediations ended up going back in front of the judge, so I decided to "lean in to it."

I ended up mediating, getting licensed, doing a little estate planning here and there, and I even went on to run a paralegal program at a college, which I also thoroughly enjoyed. I always, however, had this little bug in my ear encouraging me to open my own business one day. Eventually that little bug in my ear got louder and louder and convinced me to take a big risk, the kind of risk that scares the poop out of you because if you fail, the years of sacrifice (and little bit of savings you've managed to put together) will all be for nothing. I also had the faith and support of my husband, which was both amazing and terrifying, as I didn't want to let him down. Not to mention, I also had my son, who was a whopping one and a half years old at that point. So, I kind of, like, *really* needed this business thing to work out.

Fortunately, my very supportive, amazing husband allowed me to take all our savings and move our family to Chicago, Illinois (where I'm originally from) to start my own law practice. I was chomping at the bit to take all the skills I had learned and create a firm focused on helping young families in a more modern way.

It was then that the Law Offices of Cindy K. Campbell was born. I sought to create a firm that helped families at various stages in their lives, covering adopting a child, creating their wills and protecting their family's inheritance, creating and filing an LLC, and obtaining guardianship over an aging parent.

I had the Law Offices of Cindy K. Campbell for about five years, at which point I decided to combine forces with a friend, Joanna Long, who had her own law practice complementary to mine. In 2019, we created Campbell Long and have continued to grow our vision of helping young families in a modern, relaxed, and approachable way.

If you would like to learn more about our services, you can check out our website at CLCounsel.com.

Now that you know who I am, let's talk about some cool new ways legal services are evolving. But first…

PART I
DON'T DIY YOUR LEGAL

THE PROBLEM WITH DIY

I am the wisest man alive, for I know one thing,
and that is that I know nothing.

-Plato, The Republic

I have many clients say to me at the end of our meeting, "Wow, I'm so glad I came to see you. I didn't know any of this!"

Well, of course they didn't! Why would they?

They could have Googled the topic, which was enough to know there was some reason to see me. Or maybe they heard from a friend that there was a reason to see me. Or maybe they thought they could do it themselves and tried to file and present their own case in court...and only then did they realize there was a reason to see me.

Because we have so much information fully available at our fingertips, there is a growing trend to take a do-it-yourself (DIY) approach to everything. This allows everyday individuals to become instant professionals in the fields of everything from plumbing, medicine, to law. The problem is, there is no substitute for the years of training and education that were put into becoming a professional. Don't get me wrong, I am all for figuring out how to drain my own pipes or treat a cold, but if I have to get a cavity filled, I'm going to see my dentist.

If you think I am telling you not to DIY your legal stuff just because it hurts my industry, well, yes, part of that is true. However, the bigger reason is that it actually creates more of a mess for you to clean up. Clients who try the DIY path first later come to me and are upset. They have spent money and time doing it on their own only to find out it was done incorrectly, then *I* get to tell them it is going to cost even *more* money, take *more* time, and possibly have a worse outcome than it would have had they just done it the right way to begin with.

For example, let's say you create a will on your own by selecting an array of options from a do-it-yourself online service, but it's not correctly signed (by two uninterested witnesses, or whatever is necessary in your state). Guess what? That will is invalid. What does that mean? Your estate could pass intestate (meaning, without making a will[1]) and, according to your state's laws, not to your wishes. Just for fun, let's say there is a married couple with two children in Illinois and they do not have any valid wills in place. One spouse passes, leaving an account without a beneficiary named or having the other spouse on the title. Half of that account will go to the spouse, and the other half will be split between the two children. To make it even worse, the surviving spouse/parent cannot just step in and access the money for the children. *Au contraire mon frère*—instead, Hubby would be in court to obtain guardianship over his own kids (yes, even if he is the natural, biological parent of the children) and then would have to keep an accounting on the assets that passed to the children, making court appearances, and other not so fun stuff.

Sounds like a hot mess, right? It is! All because the couple didn't want to meet with an attorney for an hour and spend the money to make sure their wills were done correctly.

The ironic part is, we'll shell out thousands of dollars on a Louis Vuitton bag, but when it comes to making sure that our families are protected, we'll opt for an easier and/or cheaper way out. I'm guessing it is because some do not realize the value in it, but I'm here to tell you: there is *real value in it.*

I'm old school (not *that* old school, more like *Frank the Tank* old school) in that I actually try to meet in-person with all my clients. That is because when I meet with clients, I am assessing their *whole* situation, and then strategically figuring out the best way to accomplish their goals. Every matter is a little different, and that is why I need to ask questions and fully understand what the client's goals and intentions are. Only then I can help develop a plan to achieve those unique and specific goals. I prefer face-to-face or Zoom meetings because I pick up social cues and body

---

[1] *Intestate,* Black's Law Dictionary, (2nd ed, 2021).

language from the client, which I may miss in a phone interview. Don't get me wrong—sometimes, meeting in person or over Zoom is not available, and I will do phone appointments in those cases, but when I can, I try to meet with clients in person or see them live.

The reason I'm telling you this is to highlight the significance and importance of meeting with actual, live attorneys. We may live in a world where brick and mortar is not as desired, but there are still some old-school ways that stand the test of time. Finding and meeting with a lawyer, either in person or virtually, is one of them. Choosing your legal options like a fast food meal is not.

So, I am here to tell you this is not a DIY legal book. If you are looking for that, check out the NOLO series on how to do almost anything. There are also a number of legal aids out there who are staffed with lawyers and/ or law students, who may be able to help. If you are unsure where to find those, you can call your local bar associations and local law schools which may have a free or low bono legal clinic.

Instead, this is a book to help you realize when you *need* to see a lawyer, and when you don't. It's written to help you know when it may be useful to speak to a lawyer on general issues that most of us will face. This book will give you background information and terminology in your pocket, so when a situation arises in your life—like a baby, or an aging parent, or a divorce—you know where to start. This is important because there are preventative options that can be used to help client matters before they get worse. This is just one of the ways that lawyers can help.

One of my friends once told me that I'm lucky because I know how to protect myself in all sorts of situations before they arise. I realized, she's right! Although I would still go see a lawyer to help me with a particular issue, I know what to do initially and who I need to see. It was then that I decided this information could be helpful to others, and so this book was created.

IT'S A WHOLE NEW WORLD

R ight now, we are in the middle of some progressive shifts in the legal field as to how practitioners are offering services. Of course, there is still the traditional (and most common) way of hourly billing by a law firm. This is where the firm takes a retainer, which is a fee that the lawyer collects at the beginning of the representation. It is usually either a rough estimate of what the lawyer anticipates the matter may cost or the minimum amount of what the lawyer needs to have on hand in order to agree to represent the client. Upon receiving the retainer payment, the lawyer places the retainer money into a client trust account, which is a non-interest bearing account. If the lawyer is billing at an hourly rate, then as the lawyer works on the case, he or she will deduct the hourly fees from the retainer account. Once the retainer is depleted, the lawyer may ask the client to replenish the retainer account. This can be scary for the client, since they do not know how much the fees will ultimately end up costing them in the end. On the flip side, the hourly fee is usually broken down into small increments, such as one tenth of an hour (every six minutes) and so the client is only billed for the amount of time *actually* worked on the matter. In addition, for every bit of time the client is billed, the firm should give a description of the services provided during that time. So, if I researched a client issue for six minutes, it will state that. Conversely, the lawyers can't bill for getting a coffee and checking Facebook every hour, etc. This is important, because you can track and make sure the attorney's fees are "reasonable." That is, "reasonable, in relation to how much time they spent on completing the task," not, "reasonable, as in how much you *want* to pay."

If you don't agree with the time and think it is excessive, you have options. First of all, you can bring it to the lawyer's attention and sometimes the lawyers may review and make adjustments. Second, depending on what type of case or matter it is, sometimes lawyers have to present an accounting to the court and show all of the hours worked, with a detailed description of what those hours consisted of, and the judge has to approve it, in order for the attorneys to get paid.

The Shift Away from Hourly Billing

Flat Fees

There are lawyers and whole firms (like mine) that are moving toward legal services being done at a flat fee. This shift is thanks to clients and firms wanting more transparency in what legal services are going to cost upfront. This includes everything from a simple will to full blown litigation and trial.

Now, just because it's flat does not mean you are always going to like the fee. Mercedes Benz gives you a flat fee and it's not cheap, but at least you know what the price is before you decide to drive off the lot with it. Showing the customer the fee allows the customer to decide if it's worth that value ahead of time. Similarly, the client in a legal matter can look at the experience of the attorney, the trust in them, and the relationship to determine if it is worth the amount the attorney is charging. If they're not a good fit, the client can look around to find an attorney that is.

Unbundled Services

Other ways lawyers are offering alternatives to traditional representation is through unbundled legal services. Essentially, this means that instead of the lawyers taking on the case from start to finish, they just help with a part—or parts—of it. They can help you break it down into components and inform you of which parts you absolutely *need* a lawyer for. They will then let you handle the rest on your own.

In that case, a lawyer may file and only do what is called "limited scope representation." In other words, the lawyer is just stepping into the case for that *limited scope*. For example, maybe the client files the case Pro Se (which means, they choose to represent themselves), but wants to ask the lawyer to attend an upcoming hearing on reducing child support. The lawyer can just advise on that one issue and file an appearance on that one issue. In this example, the attorney would not be taking on the full case or be obligated to help with any other issues. The lawyer is simply helping by advising and appearing on that one particular issue.

Sliding Scale

Some law firms will use a sliding scale fee structure. As the name implies, the fee depends on how much you make. For example, clients who can afford to pay the going hourly rate of $500 an hour will pay that. Conversely, the client who is struggling to fill up their gas tank is going to pay a lower rate. FYI, this is usually based on the client's gross annual income, not on how much discretionary income you have and *want* to pay the attorney.

Subscription Based

Yet another way firms have become more progressive is subscription-based billing. Some firms offer a flat monthly rate, usually based on the complexity of the client's needs. I have heard of attorneys doing this for everything from landlord tenant issues to divorce.

To illustrate how this works, let's say it's your dream to start your own business but you want legal help setting up the Employment Agreements, creating and filing the LLC, creating the Operating Agreement, reviewing the lease you are going to obtain, etc. You also want an attorney you can reach with questions on your new business who can handle any of the potential problems that may arise. The subscription-based model would allow you to pick up the phone and talk with your attorney on any of these issues at the already-paid fee under your monthly subscription plan.

All of this to say, there are lawyers out there who can help all sorts of clients in all types of situations, so don't be afraid to use them!

Another thing I want to mention is the development of cool incubators with the mission of helping middle-income clients. This is for people who don't qualify for legal aid, but also don't have the ability to pay for the big firms or higher legal fees. These incubators can promote the fee structures of those stated above. Personally, I am a proud alumnus of the Justice Entrepreneurs Project, based out of Chicago, Illinois and founded by the Chicago Bar Foundation. You can find out more about it here: https://chicagobarfoundation.org/jep/. It consists of attorneys handling everything from creating your very own not-for-profit to helping with DUIs.

I give you this information in hopes that you see how the legal field has shifted to meet client demands. Attorneys are more easily accessible nowadays and they offer a greater array of fee options than ever before, so the next time you are in need of some legal help, don't be afraid to look up and see what the options are.

Summary

In summary, if you are in need of legal services and the thought of the hourly bill gives you anxiety, here are some alternative ways legal services can be delivered and billed:

- Flat fees (know the total fee up front)
- Unbundled services (only pay and use an attorney for a part of your matter)
- Sliding scale (the fee is based on your income)
- Subscription based (pay an agreed upon monthly fee for legal services)
- Check out local bar associations and law schools to see if they have any legal referral services

Now onto what I consider to be one of the most important things a parent can do to protect his or her family.

PART II
FROM BABIES TO AGING PARENTS

Whether you are taking care of little ones, taking care of aging parents, or even just managing your own everyday affairs, it can be a lot of work. This plus the daily grind make it easy to push aside getting our estate planning affairs in place or talking about it with our aging parents. But by being proactive, you can greatly impact the amount of stress you and/or your family has to deal with in the event of an emergency or tragic event.

YOU BETTER CHECK YO SELF, BEFORE YOU WRECK YO SELF

-Ice Cube

Estate Planning is not what you think!

I've had clients come to me and say, "I don't really *have* an estate!"

Well, do you own property? Like, any property at all? If so, then you do have an estate. By property I mean real and personal. According to Black's Legal Dictionary, *real property* is, "a term that is applied to land and immovable property on land such as buildings.[2]" In layman's terms, this means *land,* AKA *your house, condo,* etc. If you're thinking the bank actually owns your real property because you have a mortgage, well, that's kind of true. But, even though you may have a mortgage on the property, the title to that property should be in your name.

Personal property, conversely, is everything else other than real property. Or, according to Black's dictionary, "the belongings of an individual, *excluding* any real property or other buildings."[3] So if you own a house, a checking account, a savings account, a life insurance policy, a car, and everything in between, *you have an estate.* Therefore, you should do some planning with it.

---

[2]   *Real Property,* <u>Black's Law Dictionary</u>, (2nd ed, 2021).
[3]   *Personal Property,* <u>Black's Law Dictionary</u> (2nd ed, 2021).

When attorneys are talking about estate planning, they are generally referring to a combination of a few different documents. These most commonly consist of a will, possibly a trust (usually a Revocable Living Trust, but this can also consist of an irrevocable trust as well), Durable Powers of Attorney, and Health Care Powers of Attorney. Along with Health Care Powers of Attorney, there are other ancillary documents, such as HIPAA Waivers, and possibly Living Wills you may also consider. A Living Will is often confused with a Last Will, but they are not the same thing[4].

I'll start with the document I feel is one of the most important—and that every parent should do.

❙ Wills

The real world is not what is portrayed on television or in the movies. I know, shocker, right? In the movies, when someone dies, you may see a family sitting around and playing a video that shows the now-deceased person spelling out their wishes. This is not a "will," nor does it have any real legal significance.

A "will," otherwise known as a Last Will and Testament, is a legal document which states to whom you want your estate to pass to, successor Guardians to care for minor children, and the person who will administer the estate. Being that a will nominates Guardians, wills are a *must* for parents of young children.

Let me repeat that: wills are a *MUST* for parents of young children.

A will nominates the Guardian, who would be the person to step in and care for the child(ren) in the event the parent was not able to do so. Of all of the documents to be discussed, only the will names successor Guardians if the parents pass on.

A Guardian can be the Guardian of the estate and/or Guardian over the person. "Guardian over the person" refers to the person who will care for the child, feed them, get them to school, etc. The "Guardian of the estate" is the person handling the financial assets for the children, including

---

[4]   If you don't know what any of the documents I just mentioned are, don't worry, all of these will be defined later in this book. Keep reading!

paying for the food, clothing, etc. The same person can be both Guardian over the person and Guardian of the estate, but it does not have to be.

Why is it so important to appoint a Guardian? Because if you do not, the court will! Yes, the court will determine who will be the Guardian over your children, *not* you. Let's say Brother Bob lives closest in geographic location to the children and Sister Suz lives farthest away but has the same parenting style, similar views on raising children, and has more in common with you. You love them both dearly, but by God, you would definitely prefer that if something happened to you, the children would be raised by Sister Suz. You've never openly told them this, as you didn't want to have that awkward conversation with them. Unfortunately, because it was uncomfortable, you also never created a will, so the court has to determine the person the children should go with.

Both of the loving siblings are kind and caring enough to petition the court to be appointed as Guardian. The court does not know your preference, because nothing was ever written down. The court looks at the fact that if they stay with brother Bob, they'll be closer to their friends and more familiar with the area. Therefore, the court feels it is in the best interests of the children to appoint Brother Bob as the Guardian.

The court also does not know that you loathe Brother Bob's witch wife, and now your children will be raised by her as well. Okay, am I painting a bad enough picture yet?

Actually, this scenario is not that bad. A worse scenario is that *no one* petitions the court to be appointed as Guardian, and the children are then placed into foster care. I'm pretty sure this is every parent's worst nightmare.

I've had people tell me that because they cannot figure out the person they want to name as successor Guardian, they do not create a will at all. But, as I've shown, if you don't say it, your state will! So, unless you want your state deciding who will be the Guardian over your children, write it down. You can talk with your local estate planning attorney and he or she can help give you ideas and piece it all together. Not writing down your ideas and meeting with an attorney to make sure they're properly recorded can easily tear up the family and make a real mess of things.

Since I mentioned it, let me also make a plug here for making sure your will is properly executed. Every state has their own laws on how to create a valid Last Will and Testament. Some states require two witnesses, some accept one witness and a notary, some accept holographic wills, others do not, the list goes on. One of the benefits of meeting with an attorney is to make sure it complies with the laws of your state. I say this because I have met with clients who showed me their DIY wills that were not properly executed because they didn't have anyone guiding them on that part of the process. Thank goodness nothing ever happened to them, because those wills would have been considered invalid.

Moral of the story: when you do a will, do it right.

An Ethical Will

Sometimes clients would like to leave more than just a legal document naming their Executors and Guardians. Therefore, they may want to create an "Ethical Will," where they leave information about experiences, family lessons or traditions, and stories that were meaningful throughout their lifetime. This is a nice remembrance to leave for loved ones.

Although it is not that common, it can be a nice thing to do. When clients ask me about it, we leave a section in their binders to incorporate that information. This is the stuff you see on TV. It does not legally dispose of your estate, but it can be a nice way to be remembered.

Probate

A will also names the person (usually called the Executor or Personal Representative) who will wind down the estate, pay off the creditors and debts, and then eventually distribute the rest to the people you named as beneficiaries (AKA Legatees, which is someone who inherits through your will). This is called the "probate process" and every state varies in the complexity of this process. Some states make this process very simple, easy, and cost efficient. Other states can be more complicated and expensive. In states where it is more complicated and/or expensive, people often try to avoid going through the probate process and will use other estate planning documents, like Revocable Living Trusts (discussed more below), to avoid it.

A positive aspect of the probate process is that it limits the statute of limitations for how long any potential creditors can come forward and make a claim against the estate. A negative aspect can be the procedural laws the estate is obligated to follow, such as publishing notice in the newspapers, appearing in court, preparing accountings for the court, etc.

In some states, attorneys are required for probate. As far as the time, it can take anywhere from six months to several years to go through the probate process. The fees can range from a few thousand dollars to a percentage of the entire estate. This will depend on the state in which the estate is probated in and the complexity of it.

Some of the options for naming an Executor or Personal Representative of your estate can include a family member, a friend, a bank or corporate trustee, a Certified Public Accountant (CPA), or a lawyer (Note: "Executor" is pronounced like "executive" but with an "or" instead of the "ive" at the end—not like you are going to execute someone!). Generally speaking, you want the Executor to be equipped at handling finances, responsible, and willing to go through the probate process on your estate's behalf. You are asking this person to handle some or all of the following: accountings, the IRS, the local DMV, real estate transactions, estate sales, awkward family battles, and court. They may also deal with nasty court battles and could potentially be winding up this estate for some time, so I suggest naming someone who is comfortable being in this role.

Side note: being an Executor of an estate is a lot of work, and you will definitely want to discuss this with the person you are intending to name. People are usually shocked at how much work is involved in being an Executor. The duties may include finding all the paperwork for the deceased, notifying the banks, notifying the DMV and social security, possibly getting the house ready and selling it, preparing and filing the tax returns for the estate, finding and paying off all of the creditors, and presenting all this information for the court to approve. I have heard clients say, "I used to think my mom liked me, but I don't know if that's still true after being named the Executor of her estate!" They mean this jokingly (I hope), but it really is A LOT of work. I want to warn you of this now, so if you have been named as one, you know what you are in for. Just do what you have to do and you will get through it. Also, you can hire professionals to help you, so you are not on your own to figure out and do everything by yourself. You can hire lawyers, CPAs, financial advisors, real estate brokers, etc. to help you in this role. Also, as a little incentive for doing this, the Executor can often charge a fee for the hours worked as the Executor. The fee comes out of the estate and will be accounted for in the final accounting presented to the court. The bad news is the fee is nominal, but at least it's some compensation for the time you have to put in.

Due to this being such a big burden, I am seeing a growing trend in using professional Executors instead of asking family members to take on this responsibility. Professional Executors will charge a fee, which varies depending on who it is (a bank, a lawyer, etc). If this is something you would like to consider, I suggest asking your estate planning attorney for recommendations and then interviewing several to find the one that is a right fit for you.

Second side note: if there is an attorney helping in the probate process, they are the *estate's* attorney. If you are a beneficiary of an estate and you suspect there is foul play going on, I suggest getting your own attorney to make sure someone is looking over everything for *your* best interest. It is common, and generally will not cost too much to have an attorney review and monitor the probate process for a beneficiary's interest.

How the Estate Gets Distributed

Most often people do a general outright distribution in their wills, meaning it is an outright gift to a named beneficiary. An example of this is something like, "I give half of my estate to my sister and half to my brother." In this case, the Executor sells the property, pays off the creditors and debts, then gives half of what is left to the sister and half to the brother. There is no continuing obligation to hold on to and distribute the assets. One and done.

Another way of distributing assets is through what is called a Testamentary Trust. It is a trust created through a will naming a trustee to hold onto and distribute assets to a beneficiary upon the death of the person creating the will. The estate will still go through the probate process as mentioned above, but instead of the money going outright to a person, it will be held in a trust for them for a certain amount of time.

Why would someone do this? Well, let's say that you want to give your money to your child but you do not want her to receive it until she is at least through with college. By creating a Testamentary Trust in your will, if you were to pass before she reached let's say the age of 22, then instead of $100,000 going to her outright, it would be used for her benefit and pay college tuition, etc. until she turns 22. At that point, she would receive the remainder of her inheritance outright and could do whatever she wanted to do with it. This is just an example, and there are many more options in creating a Testamentary Trust and the distribution ages that are available.

Yet another way is to have a Revocable Living Trust (hereinafter referred to as "RLT") in place and to have your will reference your RLT and have it pass according to what the RLT states. In that case (assuming all your assets were placed correctly into the RLT), it will take your estate out of the probate court and it will all be handled privately outside of court.

MAKE SURE to Align your Accounts with Your Intentions in Your Will!!

If you are using a will to distribute the assets, the most important thing is to make sure the accounts align with what your will states. Here is an example. Let's say there is rich Uncle Scrooge who has three adoring nephews, Huey, Louie, and Dewey. Uncle Scrooge decides he will leave his big brokerage account to his three nephews, equally. He creates a will that states all of his estate will pass to these three nephews in equal shares. He then names the oldest one, Huey, as the first listed Executor in his will. The second oldest nephew, Dewey, is listed as the successor Executor to Huey. Lastly, Louie, the youngest nephew is listed as the third Executor. This means that if the first two named Executors cannot act, he will step in and act as Executor. Uncle Scrooge then uses that same list in the order described to name beneficiaries of his large brokerage account. He tells his nephews on his deathbed that he has taken care of all three of them equally.

Unfortunately, what Uncle Scrooge did was give all his entire account to Huey, his oldest nephew, making one nephew very rich and leaving his other two nephews with nothing. Because a will applies to accounts that *do not* have a named beneficiary or joint account holder, the account was not distributed according to his will. Instead, it was distributed to the named beneficiary on the account and Huey was listed as that beneficiary. If Uncle

Scrooge had named all three of them equally, the account would have passed to the three nephews in equal proportions. Or if he had named no one as a beneficiary, it would have passed under his will and passed to all three nephews equally. Unfortunately, Uncle Scrooge successfully managed to divide the family and tear them apart by not meeting with an estate planning attorney and making sure the estate would pass according to his wishes.

The moral of this story is to please, *please* meet with an estate planning *attorney* (not your financial advisor who took an estate planning seminar) and follow the attorney's recommendations on how to achieve your desired goals. A financial advisor will be well-versed in how to manage the finances, but an estate planning attorney is well-versed in making sure they pass as intended.

That being said, even if your accounts are aligned with your will, sometimes just using a will can still cause delay. Let me paint another picture for your mind: Mom and Dad had their first child. They did what they should have and created a will and purchased a large life insurance policy (the general rule of thumb I have heard is making sure there is enough cash in the policy to at least pay off the house, so the surviving parent could afford to stay with the child in their home. I'm not a financial advisor, though, so please go with whatever yours recommends for you). The parents have enough life insurance so that, in case anything were to happen to either of them, once the life insurance policy pays out, the Guardian over the child will have enough money to provide for the health and well-being of the child. The parents (on the advice of the financial advisor) named each other as primary beneficiaries on their life insurance policies and the child as the contingent beneficiary. This isn't bad, per se.

Unfortunately, something happened to the parents and because the child was still a minor, she did not have the power and could not access the proceeds of the large life insurance policy mom and dad left. The Guardian is not the named beneficiary, so the Guardian cannot immediately gain access to those funds, either. The Guardian *will* eventually get access, but he/she will need to petition the probate court to gain access to that life insurance policy—and that could take months. During those months, the Guardian will be stressed and strapped for cash.

Now I will paint a different picture: the parents met with an estate planning attorney and financial advisor. Together, they decided to establish a life insurance policy for the parents and create a RLT to hold and manage the funds for the child. They listed their trust as the beneficiary of their life insurance policies. Same situation as before, but the trustee they named steps in and immediately starts accessing the funds in the trust for the beneficiary's health, education, maintenance, and support. No court involvement is needed, and there is quick and easy access to the funds.

The other reason why many people like to use RLTs is because they help the estate avoid probate. There are certain things that need to be done when someone passes, whether they are going through probate, winding down an estate, or working through a trust. Those things consist of paying taxes (yes, as they say, the two things you cannot avoid are death and taxes—unfortunately, they are right) and paying off the debts and creditors for the decedent.[5] Going through probate will cost the estate money. Some of the fees may include filing fees, attorney's fees, publishing fees, etc.[6] By using an RLT, the estate may avoid some of those fees because the estate does not have to publish notice in the newspapers, pay an attorney to appear in court, etc. So essentially, the same general stuff has to happen, but it can be done without the pressure of having to file and appear in court or present accountings to the judge. This could save the estate a lot of money, as some states give the attorneys a flat percentage of the estate they are probating.

Summary

In summary, here are some takeaways about wills:

- It names a Personal Representative or Executor
- It names Guardians over minor or disabled children
- An Ethical Will can be a supplementary document to state wishes, intentions, traditions. It does not have legal significance and is not in lieu of a Last Will

---

[5]   A deceased person; one who has lately died. *Decedent,* Black's Law Dictionary (2nd ed, 2021).

[6]   The fees are subject to the jurisdiction.

- Probate is the court process of winding down the estate
- The will states who the estate should pass to, after paying off the taxes, debts, court fees, attorney fees, etc.

I think we've gone on enough about probate now, so let's move onto the details of living trusts.

ONLY RICH PEOPLE
NEED A TRUST

A Revocable Living Trust (RLT) is "The agreement that relates how the property of an individual is to be distributed during their lifetime and after their death."[7] With an RLT, the grantor (or the person creating the trust), will also usually be the trustee (meaning the person managing the trust). A trustee is "The person appointed, or required by law, to execute a trust; one in whom an estate, interest, or power is vested, under an express or implied agreement to administer or exercise it *for the benefit or to the use of another.*"[8] In layman's terms, the trustee manages the estate for the benefit of another.

The person creating a Grantor Trust is usually the person who is managing it, which is what most people want (to have their cake and eat it too). That means even though you have placed your assets in a trust (a critical and very important step in creating a trust), you still have full control over those assets. You can still buy and sell your property, open and close accounts, etc., but if something happens to you, the successor trustee will be able to step in and manage those assets for the beneficiaries of the trust.

Who is the beneficiary you ask? Well, that can be *you*, if you are still alive! For example, let's say that you one day develop Alzheimer's and need someone to be able to pay your bills, your taxes (yes, damn taxes again), buy you some new clothes, etc. The trustee would be able to step in and manage your assets for your benefit. Once you pass, the next listed person you named as the beneficiary is the trust's beneficiary. That can be your

---

[7]   *Revocable Living Trust,* Black's Law Dictionary (2nd ed, 2021).
[8]   *Trustee,* Black's Law Dictionary (2nd ed, 2021).

spouse, your children, or whomever you want. You can also do things in your trust like name your spouse first while he or she is alive and, once the spouse passes, then the children are the primary beneficiaries.

Administration

One of the biggest differences between an RLT and a Testamentary Trust (as mentioned above) is that you have to fund an RLT. This just means that you have to put your assets in it. I like to use the analogy of a shell (because my head always goes to water, oceans, and sipping margaritas on the beach). An RLT is like a shell that says all of the assets in the shell will be distributed as stated. But, if nothing is in there, it's kind of all for nothing. You just have an empty shell! The moral of the story is: it's really important after the trust is created to make sure it is properly funded. This will also make the administration process smoother, because the trustee will have immediate access to the assets held in the trust rather than needing to use the court to obtain such powers. Conversely, to fund a Testamentary Trust, the estate will have to involve the court in order to get the trust funded.

I'm not going to lie, the funding portion of an RLT can be a *pain!* If you create a trust you will be tasked with going to all of your existing accounts and retitling your assets or changing the beneficiaries on the accounts. If it's any consolation, it is much easier than it used to be. Nowadays, most institutions are pretty well versed in trusts and have a "change of beneficiary" form online you can download and use. The most important thing after you have created a trust is that you have funded it and that it is funded correctly. If it's not funded correctly, you can run into a host of problems, so make sure to speak with your attorney about properly funding it. It is critical that you do this step, because if you do not, it will pass outside of the trust and through probate.

Here comes another horror story to drive home the point: let's say Mom and Dad create a trust through a one-size-fits-all, estate-planning, document-generating business that pops out some sort of trust and will for them. The problem is, now we have the "shell" with nothing in it. A new deed was never created transferring their real property into their shell (AKA their trust). Due to the time, a lack of general knowledge, and not being informed on where to go for help or even what is needed, Mom and Dad leave everything out of the shell but their life insurance policy. The good thing is, the life insurance will pass according to their wishes. The bad thing is, the rest of their estate will go through probate. Depending on what their will states, if it was even executed correctly, the rest of their estate may be administered completely different from their intentions and have an outright distribution to the kids at a young age. The parents created this beautiful trust and then failed to do the most important step of funding it.

Side note: if you fear this may be your story, ask an attorney to review your trust and/or the funding! I have had clients come to me with estate planning documents and trusts that were drafted years ago, but for which a deed was never prepared or signed to make sure their property passed according to their trust. Your local estate planning attorney can easily create a deed and record it, if necessary.

Side note two: many firms can do the funding for you. Just ask! Most firms can help you transfer your financial accounts into your trust and create and record deeds transferring your real property into your trusts. Or, if you work with a financial advisor, he or she can help transfer your financial assets into the trust and have the attorney help with the real estate.

When you are transferring real estate into a trust, you will want to record a deed (this could be a Deed in Trust, a Quit Claim Deed, or a Transfer on Death Instrument, to name a few)[9]. You can try doing this yourself or hire your local estate planning attorney who can advise on what type of deed is appropriate and should be able to create the deed and record it for you—but I want to mention that some states and cities are not as easy to record deeds in. I have recorded deeds in a variety of cities and states, and each one has its own specific requirements—which is even more the reason why you need your local attorney or title company to do this part. Cities and states vary on the recording fees and attorney's fees for accomplishing this, but trust me, it's worth it. It's a huge pain, and it's something you want to pay people who do this all the time to do for you.

Okay, so let's assume that you created an RLT and funded it correctly. Now the trustee steps in and starts accessing the assets within the trust for

---

[9]   These are all different types of deeds and can depend on the state you reside in and the attorney's recommendations.

the benefit of the beneficiaries. There are a number of ways to structure the distribution scheme and determine who should inherit your estate. There are all sorts of ways to be creative in them, too, if that is what you desire. Here are a few options.

Distributions

First, let me state that at the very least, the trustee will provide for the beneficiaries' health, education, maintenance, and support (HEMS). This is often referred to as the "HEMS" standard. What does this look like in everyday life? The trustee will pay for all the day-to-day living expenses such as housing, clothes, food, activities, etc. If the beneficiaries are not receiving their distributions until later in life, the trustee may also be paying for college tuition, books, room, board…you get the point. You can also go beyond the HEMS standard and allow the trustee to distribute it for any purpose. This is something you should discuss with your attorney.

The way in which your estate is distributed will also depend on who is receiving it. For example, you may not put the same restrictions on the funds for your spouse as you do your children.

Spouses

With spouses, you can give it all to the spouse with a general power of appointment, meaning the spouse can do whatever they want to do with it. Or, you can give it all to them to use during their lifetime under the HEMS standard—meaning they can use it for health, education, maintenance, and support—and have it so that after the spouse passes, it then goes to the children under the terms stated for them. You can also give a portion to the spouse and a portion to be held in the trust for the benefit of the kids and then, when the spouse passes, whatever is left goes to the children. You may also want to give it all to the spouse but create different "buckets" (or sub trusts created in the trust) from which the spouse receives distributions to avoid tax consequences. This, of course, will depend on your intentions and what is a priority for you. Is your highest priority ease of administration, protection from creditors, or avoiding taxes? All of these should be considered in determining how the trust will be created.

Children

With the children, there are more potential events to consider. You may want to consider their youth and inexperience with handling money. You don't want your kids to inherit a boat load at twenty-one and spend it all by twenty-two. Luckily, there are a number of ways to structure the distributions so that does not happen.

Again, the trustee will manage the assets in the RLT for the children's benefit and give to them for HEMS and anything else you add. They may also give to them for any purpose if that is what you choose, or you may choose to limit the distributions. You can tell the trustee you want him to be liberal in his distributions and encourage world travel, etc. Conversely, you can have conservative distributions if you want to instill a hard work ethic, and insist the money should only be distributed in accordance with that goal. Or, you could hold it all in a trust to be distributed only for a specific purpose, like funding education.

A family pot is a popular way to distribute assets if you have more than one child. With a family pot, you can hold the children's inheritance in "one pot" until the children get through college. Then, once every child is through college or has attained a certain age, the children's sub trusts get funded and they can start receiving their distributions.

Another popular distribution method is holding it all in the trust until the *trustee* decides they are responsible enough to handle that kind of money. In that case, maybe you allocate the income to the children to do what they want with it, but the principal is only distributed at the trustee's discretion.

Yet another popular distribution method is by sprinkling the children's distributions throughout their lifetimes and not giving them too much at one time. For example, the trustee can distribute a certain percentage at a certain age or upon graduating from college. In this scenario, let's say the trustee will distribute 10 percent at twenty-three or upon graduating from college with a four-year degree, whichever occurs first. Then they get 25 percent at twenty-six, and then the remainder upon reaching thirty years of age. This preserves most of the assets until they are a little older, but still gives them access to some funds earlier so they can start learning how to manage money.

Grandchildren

Trusts can also allow you to set up trusts for the next-level beneficiaries, grandchildren. You may even want to skip the kids or only give the kids a certain amount (say, up to the amount where they would be taxed) and then have the rest go down to the grandkids to be held in trust for them. Or, you may want to put a certain amount in a trust to be used for their education.

As you can see, there are lots of options. Your local attorney can help you decide which one is the right fit for you.

Predeceased Beneficiaries

What happens if one of your beneficiaries predeceases you? Well, your trust (or your will) should name contingent beneficiaries. You may want it to pass down to that beneficiary's children, or according to that person's estate. Or you may want to name charities, or specific people to inherit. Alternatively, some people just have it pass to their heirs at law, which essentially follows the bloodline. This is where I often have clients tell me they definitely don't want cousin Tony inheriting any assets, and we intentionally disinherit a blood relative on the off-chance the zombie apocalypse happened.

The Cinderella Story

The biggest reason I favor using RLTs, is because I am a mom myself, and it gives my kids more protection from the Cinderella scenario. Let me paint a picture for you: wife passes and leaves everything to her husband. Husband gets remarried and believes his new wife truly loves his children from his first marriage. They have one child of their own and they treat and love all children equally. Husband creates a new will with his new wife, wherein he gives everything to her and then to his children equally. He then sadly passes away, and the new wife inherits everything. Cue the evil laughter. New wife decides that her child really needs more of the money than the older step children. Or, she decides that her stepchildren don't come to see her as much as she wants, or she falls in love with some other man. Whatever happens, in the end, she changes her will and leaves nothing to her step children. Those step children never received anything from their loving parents and it all went to the evil step mother.

This can easily happen in a will by doing what most couples want, which is something like, "I give all to my spouse, and if he/she passes, then I give equally to my children." In theory, this distribution scheme is fine, but if you do it through a simple will, that leaves the estate vulnerable. If the surviving spouse remarries, they will have the power to give it all to the new spouse or anyone else they choose.

In all honesty, there are many people who do not and will not inherit from their parents, and it is because of this type of poor estate planning. To avoid situations like this, you can use a Revocable Living Trust (RLT) in conjunction with the will to make sure after your spouse passes, that the estate always goes to *your* children and that cannot be changed.

| Avoiding Taxes

I won't bore you with the legal details that put you to sleep (or make you regret buying this book), but there are some points I want to mention here in case they are applicable to you.

There are all sorts of ways to avoid taxes!

Now I piqued your interest, right?! Don't get too happy yet, as this is geared toward the upper 1 percent of the 1 percent. That being said, the level at which estates get taxed at fluctuates. Currently, the estate tax amount is uber-high ($12.06M and $24.12M for a couple). But, that is supposed to sunset as of 2025 and potentially go back to $5.49M and $10.90M per couple (adjusted for inflation). Still really high, but definitely has a significant drop, and is subject to change.

Okay, so rates change, but taxes are a certainty. Again, death and taxes, right? So, if you think your estate may be subject to taxes in the future, you should absolutely seek out an estate planning attorney and ask what you can do. The rate at which estates are taxed at is pretty high. Unfortunately, if you meet the taxable threshold, you can expect to be taxed at up to 40 percent, and that's just the federal tax. Some states tax, too, and they may have a much lower threshold than the federal level. For example, in the states of Oregon and Massachusetts, if you have over $1,000,000 in assets at the time of death, you will be hit with state "death tax." Luckily, there are ways for attorneys to structure revocable and irrevocable trusts to avoid taxes. Some of them are: Disclaimer Trusts, Marital Deduction Trusts, Qualified Terminal Interest Property Trusts (QTIPs), and Generation Skipping Trusts (GSTs), to name a few. These are clauses that can be added into your revocable trust that will not kick into effect until after the grantor passes. Irrevocable trusts can also be used to help to move money now to avoid estate taxes later.

Irrevocable Trusts.

While most of the time clients want revocable trusts, there are times when an irrevocable trust is more appropriate and/or should be used in conjunction with an RLT. Some types of *irrevocable trusts* include: Special Needs Trusts, Medicaid Trusts, Irrevocable Life Insurance Trusts, and Gift Trusts, to name a few.

Special Needs Trusts

A Special Needs Trust can be beneficial when parents have a special needs child and want to provide for that child after they pass, and also ensure their child will still be able to receive government benefits. Medical expenses can be very *costly*, which is not something that is surprising to anyone living in the United States. A few trips to the hospital, daily medication, therapy, etc. can easily dwindle down even large estates. The good news is, there is a way to ensure that the special needs child will be able to retain the government benefits, and their inheritance can supplement their needs. That is through what is called either a Special Needs Trust or a Supplemental Needs Trust, depending on jurisdiction. This is an irrevocable trust that names a trustee to manage the money for the disabled beneficiary. This can be accomplished through either a stand-alone Special Needs Trust or one that will be created through the RLT.

If you think this could be beneficial to you or a loved one, I suggest asking your local attorney about it. These can be complicated, and you will want to make sure it meets all your state's requirements.

Medicaid Trusts

This is a hot topic with the baby boomers. A Medicaid trust can help shield assets so Mom or Dad can qualify for Medicaid later in life. This can be useful if you think there is a possibility of Mom or Dad ending up in a skilled nursing home at some point in the future. This is an irrevocable trust, and Mom and/or Dad have to give up their rights to control or benefit from their assets. Instead, they must name a third party to manage all their assets, and a third party has the right to benefit from their assets. The grantor (Mom or Dad in this case) will still receive the income generated from their assets, but will not be able to go in and use the principal for their benefit. Also, in some states, there is a five-year look back period on transferring assets into the trust.

These are complicated and state specific. If this is something you think may be needed in your family at some point, you will need to see an estate planning or elder law attorney who can help you with it. They are usually quite costly, but can also save the estate hundreds of thousands of dollars if done correctly.

Irrevocable Life Insurance Trusts

This is more commonly referred to as an ILIT. An ILIT is a tool that can be used to minimize estate taxes, wherein the client will put a life insurance policy in the irrevocable trust. Because it is in an irrevocable trust and the grantor (the person creating and funding the trust) is not the named beneficiary (and the grantor is giving up the power and control over such an asset), it will not be counted as part of the estate. So, when the taxman comes later on down the road to collect, that $1,000,000 life insurance policy will not be taxed at the estate tax level, or even considered in the taxable estate. Since it is not part of the estate, a client may also want to create and fund this to be used to pay the estate taxes later.

For example, let's say Mom has $12,700,000 to leave to Daughter. Because Daughter would be taxed at 40 percent for the $1,000,000 over the federal exemption amount (which at the time I'm writing this is currently $11,700,000) she could purchase and fund an ILIT for $1,000,000 to move money out of her estate. Then, her estate would not be taxed at the federal level.

Gift Trust

A gift trust is similar to an ILIT in that the intention is generally to move money out of the grantor's estate, and the grantor is not the named beneficiary. As the name implies, the grantor is gifting an asset to someone and giving up any rights and benefits to and from that asset. By doing this, it will not be counted as part of the grantor's estate. There is a limit on how much a person can gift over their lifetime, and that is currently the federal tax level.

Other things to Consider

If you are a foreign citizen, you may want/need to consider Qualified Domestic Trust. The government wants to make sure that a non-citizen spouse doesn't run off with all of the money and not give any to the United States. Shocking, right? So, to make the IRS happy, we can use a Qualified Domestic Trust. Whether there is over $2,000,000 in said trust determines how it will be administered. It is a little more complicated and may require a co-trustee who is a US Citizen to be appointed to act with the surviving spouse/trustee. This may or may not be needed in your situation, so ask your attorney to assess whether it's right for you.

Summary of Trusts

To recap, here are some of the benefits and reasons to do a trust, both revocable and irrevocable:

- A Trustee manages the assets in a trust
- Trusts give more protection against creditors
- There is more protection around ensuring the estate passes to the intended beneficiaries
- Is private
- Avoids probate
- Maximizes tax exemptions
- Allows for more complex distributions to the beneficiaries
- Can help retain government benefits and assistance

While your wills and trusts provide a lot of benefits after you pass, there are some other documents that are good to have in your reservoir in case you need them while you are living.

OTHER THINGS TO THINK ABOUT

Parents are always aging, and there may come a time when something happens to them and you need to step in and take care of them—or someone needs to step in and take care of you! Some important documents in estate planning when it comes to the ability to step in and act for someone are Durable Powers of Attorney and Healthcare Powers of Attorney. The power to act on someone else's behalf can apply to both financial powers and medical powers, and it can either be difficult or easy to obtain such powers. I am going to start with the financial powers and Durable Powers of Attorney (DPA).

Durable Powers of Attorney

This document appoints an "attorney-in-fact" or "agent" who is authorized to act on another's behalf. An "attorney-in-fact" is not a licensed attorney in that state, but a person acting in a fiduciary capacity for another. A fiduciary is "… a person…who is invested with the rights and powers to be exercised for the benefit of another person."[10] Translation: you are trusted to work on and in the *best interests of* someone else's behalf. A Durable Power of Attorney (hereinafter referred to as "DPA") can give your attorney-in-fact the power to access and manage the estate of another for that person's benefit.

---

[10]   *Fiduciary*, Black's Law Dictionary (2nd ed, 2021).

You may be asking, "Why would I give someone this power?" Well, you would do so if you are incapacitated or otherwise unavailable, and you would need someone to act for you.

DPAs are beneficial if you are in a temporary state of incapacity and need someone to access your accounts. Let's say, for example, that you were in a car accident and you need someone to pay the mortgage, utility bill, or even preschool fees. Your DPA would allow your attorney-in-fact the ability to step in and access your financial accounts so that he or she would have the ability to pay those bills for you. The powers you give your attorney-in-fact can be broad and expansive, or restricted and narrow. There are reasons and benefits for both.

The powers can either start immediately or they could be what we call *springing powers*. A "springing power" just means the power *springs* into action upon the happening of some event, i.e., you become incapacitated. When we are using a DPA to appoint an attorney-in-fact to act on the principal's behalf (the principal is the person creating the document) and the principal is healthy, the principal may want to use springing powers. In this case, the person the principal is appointing would not be able to act *unless* the principal was unable to act for him or herself. In that case, we generally do not put time limits on such powers and it is left open, so if the principal cannot act for years, the attorney-in-fact is able to carry out all of the necessary duties to take care of the principal's financial affairs over that time.

However, sometimes you might need these powers to be evoked immediately, even though you are perfectly healthy. An example of that would be if you are selling your house. The attorney may have you sign a DPA granting real estate powers to the attorney-in-fact. The attorney-in-fact, in this situation, could actually be your licensed attorney helping you on the matter, or someone else representing you, who would then handle and sign all the real estate documents on your behalf. In this case, the powers would likely be restricted and only for the purpose of managing real estate transactions on the principal's behalf. It would also likely be limited in its duration, to a period that is reasonable for the attorney-in-fact to carry out such responsibilities.

It is not just real estate powers that you can give your attorney-in-fact, though. Here is a list of some of the powers they can have, as listed on the Illinois Statutory Durable Power of Attorney:

- Real estate transactions
- Tangible personal property transaction
- Business operating transactions
- Personal and family maintenance
- Banking and other financial institution transactions
- Stock and bond transactions
- Commodity and option transactions
- Insurance and annuity transactions
- Claims and litigations
- Benefits from Social Security, Medicare, Medicaid, or other governmental programs, or civil or military service
- Retirement plan transactions
- Tax matters

What does this mean? Well, if the powers are broad like those shown, it can allow for the attorney-in-fact to move around assets, access insurance policies, pay off debts, sell a house, and file and pay your taxes, to name a few.

There are also some powers that have come about more recently, like access to digital assets. This would allow your attorney-in-fact the ability to set up an "out of office" for your email or put a pause on your Facebook account and make sure it does not get hacked.

Creating this document is relatively easy to do and generally inexpensive. In fact, many states have their own DPA form that can be found on the state's website. In the state of Illinois, where I reside, they provide a state Statutory DPA. That being said, it may still be useful to see an attorney to fill this out, as the attorney may add in more or less powers than what the standard state form includes. Your attorney may want to create a General DPA instead or in addition to the state form, covering powers the state form does not (like the digital assets mentioned above).

Not only are these documents important for aging parents, but they are important for *all adults!*

Off to College

Even though they will always be your "baby," once your kiddos hit the magic number of eighteen, they are now legally adults. What consequences does that have? Well for one, you will no longer have the ability to immediately step in and act for them if you need to. This is a huge mental shift for parents who are used to being able to help their kiddos with everything. These powers can include everything from talking with the landlord to deal with roommate issues to needing to pay a utility or cell phone bill. Although you have had the ability to step in and make their decisions since they were born, at the magic number of eighteen, you suddenly lose all your power. Therefore, it is super important to get a DPA in place over your adult children. Having these documents in place could literally save you many hours of frustration and expense.

Yourself

We've spoken about parents and children, but these are also really important for you! But of course, who is the last person a mom thinks about taking care of? Herself!

In the event that you are in an accident and need your spouse to be able to step in and act for you, you better get a DPA in place.

Healthcare Powers

The other power of attorney that you will want to have in place for your parents, your adult children, and yourself is Healthcare Powers of Attorney (hereinafter referred to as "HCPOA"). This is also sometimes referred to as an Advanced Healthcare Directive. As the name implies, this document allows you to appoint an agent to make healthcare decisions over you. This can also be immediate or springing. Most of the time, we create these to be springing and the agent will only step in to make healthcare decisions when the principal person cannot make them for himself or herself.

There can be times, however, where it makes sense to give immediate powers to make healthcare decisions over someone else. For example, let's say Mom has dementia. Most days she seems fine, but some days she is not. Unfortunately, this disease is only going to progress, and at some point she will no longer have the ability to create these documents as she will lack the requisite capacity. Therefore, it may make sense for Mom to give immediate powers to her agent now. That way, on the "off days" when Mom's mental state is questionable, her child can step in and act for her.

Just like with a DPA, there can be both state statutory short forms or general forms. Again, with a general form, you will usually find more custom language that expands on the provisions of the short form. For example, maybe it is your intent that you would like to stay living at home for as long as possible. Or maybe you have a specific living environment you would like, or you want to limit the organs that can be donated.

Note: this is a hot one. On your driver's license, you may state that you want to be an organ donor, but do you want it to be a full donorship? Meaning, after an immediate medical transplant, your body could be used for education. This means you could end up as a cadaver with a bunch of twenty-one-year-olds poking and prodding you. If that's your thing, cool! Someone's got to help advance our learning and technology. But, if you're thinking all the worst (like I am), you may want to state that so your agent knows to limit your organ donation.

Another popular clause in the HCPOA is to allow for palliative care. Palliative care allows you to receive medicine for pain, even if it is likely to hasten your death. This is something most people want, so if you do, make sure to speak with your attorney about adding this clause into your HCPOA.

Lastly, in a HCPOA, there is sometimes also the ability to state your Living Will decisions (see more on this below). Usually in a HCPOA, this is only a short sentence or two of when to pull the plug, though, so you may want to ask your attorney about creating a stand-alone Living Will.

Requirements

The requirements for a valid DPA and HCPOA will depend on your state, so it's important to meet with an attorney in your state to review and sign. Some states require two witnesses, while others only require one witness and a notary. Although this may feel trivial, if it's not signed correctly (two *uninterested* witnesses—possibly not even your doctor or nurse) then the whole thing is invalid.

As I mentioned, these are relatively easy-to-create and inexpensive documents, but make sure you do it right. If not, you may end up using the following means of obtaining decision making abilities over another, which is generally more time-consuming and expensive.

Guardianship/Conservatorships

If you do not have your powers of attorney in place, you're not totally SOL in regards to having someone step in and act for you. You may, however, be able to obtain guardianship or a conservatorship over the disabled adult. This is where one party is given *full* power and control over making financial decisions and/or healthcare decisions over someone else. This is more expansive than a Durable Power of Attorney and cannot be revoked by the disabled person.

Every state is different in their process and procedure for obtaining a guardianship over someone else. As you can imagine, and thank God, the court takes this very seriously. You don't want the courts stripping away someone's powers and autonomy and giving them to someone else lightly. The problem is, if you need those powers immediately, you may not get them. Sometimes, you may have to wait months just to get into court. Then there will likely be some type of Guardian Ad Litem, or "eyes and ears of the court," to interview the person, the home, the doctors, etc. before the judge will award such powers.

Once the judge approves of the guardianship over the Ward (the disabled person), the Guardian will have the ability to step in and handle all transactions on the Ward's behalf. They will need to create and follow a budget for the Ward's anticipated spending and prepare and file annual accountings to the court showing what was actually spent.

It will be a more complex process than just creating a document like a DPA, and the court will be heavily involved. Family members also have the ability and may contest the appointment if they feel the wrong Guardian was appointed and/or is acting negligently in their fiduciary duties.

In Summary

Here are some takeaways:

- Durable Powers of Attorney – allows access to manage financial affairs for another individual
- Healthcare Powers of Attorney – allows access to make healthcare decisions for another individual
- Powers of Attorney can give immediate or springing powers
- Powers of Attorney are not just for elderly people. They can be beneficial for anyone over eighteen.
- Guardianships and Conservatorships – grant full control over another and require court involvement

Okay, bear with me—there is just *one* more really important topic we should discuss when it comes to estate planning.

PULLING THE PLUG

A Living Will is a document that tells your family you want them to terminate life support ("pull the plug") if you become brain dead (AKA a persistent vegetative state or an irreversible coma) or become terminally ill and are on life support, where the benefits of any further procedures are not likely to outweigh the burdens.

Why do we have this? Well, because our country does not like the idea of letting people die. Physicians take the Hippocratic Oath (their promise to keep us alive) very seriously, which is obviously good. We want doctors to help us get better when we are sick and to help us live longer (that's kind of the whole point of doctors). The bad thing is, sometimes they keep us alive even when it's apparent the soul is ready to move on. It's in these times that a Living Will can be useful.

Back in 1983, a young woman, Nancy Cruzan, was in a car accident that left her in a persistent vegetative state. Her parents wanted to withdraw the feeding tube, but they were denied the right to do so from the Missouri Supreme Court. The parents appealed to the United States Supreme Court, and that court held that, absent *clear and convincing evidence* that Nancy wanted life support to be withdrawn, the state may constitutionally *refuse* to withdraw such treatment (*Cruzan v. Director, Missouri Department of Health*, 487 U.S. 261,1990). That's right—without clear and convincing evidence, the state may tell your family they do not have the power to make the decision of terminating life support. This, in turn, gives the power to the state (not the family) to decide if a person lives in a persistent vegetative state or not. That means a person could live for many years on a machine, unable to communicate or have a meaningful life.

In Nancy's case, there was a witness who testified Nancy had told her she did not want to live that way, and with that evidence, the parents were able to have the life support withdrawn. During that time, Nancy stayed in a persistent vegetative state and on life support for *seven years* until her parents took the issue of the "Right to Die" all the way up to the United States Supreme Court. Throughout that time her family was put through public ridicule and shame for wanting to withdraw the life support keeping her alive.

If you are wondering why a family would want to do this, know that it's not that they are cruel people who want to kill their family member. Instead, it is usually out of compassion. You see, "most" people do not want to live in a hospital bed, unable to feed themselves, bathe, go to the bathroom on their own, nor communicate, let alone live that way for many years. Yet medical technology will allow us to do so. Therefore, as an advocate for the person who is unable to communicate, the family may want to pursue terminating life support for that person.

Let me give a side note here: we are not talking about Physician Assisted Dying (PAD). That is where a doctor (does "Dr. Kevorkian" ring a bell?) actually gives you poison to help you die. In this case, we are talking about a situation where, if it were not for the life support, the patient would die. The life support is the only thing keeping the patient alive.

Let's jump now to 2005, when we have the Theresa "Terri" Shiavo case. This was the case where a 41 year old woman suffered a cardiac arrest leading to her being in a persistent vegetative state for over fifteen years. Terri collapsed in her home in 1990 and did not leave any medical directives. For the first few years the husband and her parents got along. Then they started to have problems, as apparently the husband started to see another woman. In 1998 he petitioned to have Terri's life support withdrawn.

Because this happened in Florida and she did not have an advanced directive (AKA a Living Will), there was a list in order of priority of proxies to make health care decisions for the incapacitated person. The list consisted of a judicially appointed guardian, then their spouse, then the adult children of the patient, and then the parents of the patient. Here, the spouse was higher on the list, so he was the one who ultimately got to make the decision. He and the judge held that there was *clear and convincing evidence* and determined the feeding tube should be withdrawn. Her parents felt the opposite. They filed many subsequent lawsuits to try to have the feeding resumed, claiming therapy could potentially help her.

Conversely, there were also medical experts claiming that her condition would not improve. After fifteen years and many lawsuits, eventually the feeding tube was removed.

I bring up these cases, not to convince you one way or the other on whether to terminate life support, but to make a decision about it and have it in writing. The moral of the story is to *write it down!* Seriously, it can save your family the pain, heartache, and possibly years in court that come with making these really awful decisions.

I can speak to this both professionally and personally. Not only is this an issue I discuss with clients regularly in doing their Living Wills, but right out of undergrad I also worked at a hospice for a few months. Although it was only a short time that I worked there, I learned a lot and it was definitely enlightening. I saw first hand how difficult it can be for a family to deal with Living Will decisions for a loved one. What I would see and hear is that often the family caring for the ill person knew that the patient did not want to live that way. Conversely, the extended family (not doing the day-to-day care) would feel strongly that the patient should continue to live on life support and hope for a miracle. This debate on what decisions to make for the patient can sadly put a big fat wedge between the family members. It is much easier when you don't have to make that awful decision and instead follow the patient's stated wishes.

Ironically, (being that I worked in hospice and then went into the estate planning area of legal practice), we had to invoke my own father's Living Will that I had created for him many years prior. When I created it, I naively never thought I would be using it. I mean, my grandparents lived into their nineties and my dad (except for his love of ice cream, doughnuts, pastries, and cookies, to name a few) had always been relatively healthy. The week he passed he was playing baseball with my sons in the front yard and pretending to be a horse on the ground with two little boys jumping and climbing on him.

So, you can imagine how much of a complete shock it was to hear that he suddenly went from a bad stomach ache at night to having to decide whether to terminate life support before his kidneys and other organs all started failing the next morning. It was completely awful, and one of those moments where time feels like it doesn't exist. Looking back, it was one of those bubbles, where I felt like I was out of my body, suddenly having to make very awful and serious decisions in a time when I couldn't even tell you which way was up. Truly, the only good thing was that at that moment, we didn't have to make those decisions. My dad had already done it years prior, when he created his Living Will. The guilt and pressure was not on us: the decision had already been made.

Sometimes I still question whether there was something else that could have been done—but then I stop myself and remember: it was not our decision. The decision was my father's, and he didn't just tell us in passing. Instead, he took the time to have it written down and witnessed, so there was no room for guessing his wishes. It was painful, emotional, and one of the worst moments in my life, but at least *I* didn't have to make that tough decision.

Therefore, I ask all of you to make a decision and get it in writing so there is no drama for your baby mama. If you don't, it can tear the whole family apart. Some will want to hold on for hope that the gods are going to shine down on the patient and a miracle will happen (this has actually happened before, so as crazy as it is, maybe it's not that crazy). The other part of the family will say that no one wants to live like that and we should consider the quality of life. Then there are some who are just undecided and are not sure what the person would have wanted or what to do. They have doctors on one side saying the illness cannot be reversed, but the guilt and grief make the decision unbearable. So, put this on your checklist of "adult things to do," please!

| PAD

As I mentioned, when discussing Living Wills, we are not talking about Physician Assisted Dying (PAD) or Aid-In Dying. This used to be called Physician Assisted Suicide, but now the "suicide" part has been replaced with "dying" for obvious (how flipping depressing can we make this subject?) reasons. PAD refers to when the patient has been diagnosed with a terminally ill disease and chooses to hasten his or her death before the disease completely takes over the body and the ability to make such decisions.

This is covered in the Death with Dignity Act, which not many states have adopted. Some of the states that have are: California, Colorado,

District of Columbia, Hawaii, Oregon, Vermont, Washington, and New Jersey. Oregon has been at the forefront of this movement, passing the first Death With Dignity Act in 1994. Of course, as with all laws, each state has its own requirements, so if this is something you would like more information on, I suggest reaching out to your local estate planning attorney to see what the laws are of your state and what can be done about it.

All I can say to this issue (as it is not legal in my state) is to remember that you never know what someone else is going through. In these situations, the patients are already losing a battle with their diseases and experiencing daily suffering. These acts have been enacted to bring peace to terminally ill patients. If you or a loved one are curious about this, there are some fascinating documentaries on the subject that may shed some light on the process for the patient and their families.

Summary

In summary, all of the aforementioned documents work cohesively in allowing another to act in the event of a tragedy. Each document mentioned is one piece of the estate plan. In the event of a sudden emergency or tragic event, the Durable Powers of Attorney and Healthcare Powers of Attorney allow the named agent to make necessary healthcare decisions and help with financial affairs. If there is a trust in place, the trustee named in the trust can access the accounts in the trust and use those funds for healthcare expenses, support, and care. If the person passes on, the will tells the court who everything is going to and names the guardians over the children. If there is a trust in place, the will helps get everything into the trust and then the trust states how and to whom everything is passing to, while hopefully avoiding some otherwise unnecessary burdens like estate taxes or the termination of government assistance.

Without one or all of these documents in place, the estate can still get managed but it will generally be more stressful, time consuming, and expensive to do so.

PART III
NOT WHAT YOU HOPED FOR

Sometimes life throws you a curveball and things don't work out the way you had hoped. If that happens, it's good to be prepared and know what your options are when considering divorce or working through parenting issues.

THE D WORD

We are about to enter into the chapter no one wants to enter. Yes, I'm talking about the D-word: "divorce," which, to some, may feel worse than the other D-word: "death." Our society puts a lot of pressure on staying married, but sometimes it's just not right for the couple or the family anymore. The spouses may be much happier and better people when they are not tied to a bad relationship. Often, my clients tell me that by the time they told the children they were getting divorced, the kids said, "Uh, yeah, it's pretty obvious!"

I say this because if you are going through, considering going through, or know someone who is going through a divorce, you or they are not a bad person, so please be kind to yourself, your friend, your family member, or whomever is going through it.

Divorce is scary, painful, and sad. People don't go into a marriage wanting or hoping for a divorce, but unfortunately, life is not always what we planned. As hard as some couples may work at it, it just might not be good for either party to continue in the relationship.

In addition to ending the relationship, and going through that pain, there are a whole host of issues the couple needs to sort out to end that relationship. These issues include the division of assets and debts, support issues for children and spouses, living arrangements for each spouse and the children, dividing businesses, sorting out health insurance, the list goes on. My point is, it's not easy. It's complex, and it's a lot of work. The reason people trek through this treacherous journey is because they believe life is going to be better on the other side of it.

I have met some people who have been through really awful divorces who are still in a bad place from it many years after the fact. On the flip side, I have seen former clients who come up and hug me and thank me for helping them get out of their marriage, as they have now moved on to a happy place in their lives.

Choosing the right lawyer and procedure for obtaining the divorce or parenting agreement is the key difference. The "right" path can vary depending on a number of issues, and there is not one that is right for everyone. I'll soon detail different ways to handle the process of divorce, but first I want to start with a list of some of the things that will need to be worked through no matter how you decide to proceed.

Common Issues in Divorce

No matter how you proceed with a divorce, there are certain issues the couple is going to have to work through no matter what. Here are some things to consider in every divorce, whether using traditional methods or alternative ones: division of assets and debts, alimony or maintenance, child support, visitation schedules, parenting responsibilities, allocation of household goods, taxes, and legal fees.

First, you will need to determine the grounds (i.e. the reason) for the divorce. Most states have adopted "no fault" divorces and many people take advantage of this, citing "irreconcilable differences" as the grounds for divorce. This essentially means the couple can no longer reconcile their differences and wish to part ways. Depending on the state you live in, there may be a period of time which is required for the couple to try to reconcile their differences. In Illinois, this period is six months, but even that time period may be shortened if both parties agree to waive it.

Some states provide for "at fault" divorces, where it will need to be proved who is at fault for the breakdown of the marriage. Examples of fault-based grounds are: adultery, cruelty, desertion, or impotence, to name a few. Oh, and by the way, it's not enough to say your husband is a lying cheating bastard—you'll actually need to prove it. It is also not enough to just say your bastard husband left and deserted you. You'll need to prove it. That means showing the court that he cannot be found anywhere, even through mail, text, Facebook, his family, etc.

In addition to having the burden of proving this claim, the judge may not give you more of the assets just because your husband left. So, the only thing you may get is more money spent to prove that he is a cheating bastard. That may, in itself, be worth it to you, but you should know it might not help you bring home more bacon.

Alimony or Maintenance

The start date for the calculation of alimony or maintenance is the start of the marriage. Every state is different in how they determine what is owed and to whom, but generally speaking, each state is going to consider certain factors. Here are the factors considered in Illinois:

> (1) the income and property of each party, including marital property apportioned and non-marital property assigned to the party seeking maintenance as well as all financial obligations imposed on the parties as a result of the dissolution of marriage;

> (2) the needs of each party;

> (3) the realistic present and future earning capacity of each party;

> (4) any impairment of the present and future earning capacity of the party seeking maintenance due to that party devoting time to domestic duties or having forgone or delayed education, training, employment, or career opportunities due to the marriage;

> (5) any impairment of the realistic present or future earning capacity of the party against whom maintenance is sought;

> (6) the time necessary to enable the party seeking maintenance to acquire appropriate education, training, and employment, and whether that party is able to support himself or herself through appropriate employment;

> (6.1) the effect of any parental responsibility arrangements and its effect on a party's ability to seek or maintain employment;

> (7) the standard of living established during the marriage;

> (8) the duration of the marriage;

(9) the age, health, station, occupation, amount and sources of income, vocational skills, employability, estate liabilities, and the needs of each of the parties;

(10) all sources of public and private income including, without limitation, disability and retirement income;

(11) the tax consequences to each party;

(12) contributions and services by the party seeking maintenance to the education, training, career or career potential, or license of the other spouse;

(13) any valid agreement of the parties; and

(14) any other factor that the court expressly finds to be just and equitable.

(750 ILCS 5/504).

In addition to looking at those factors, the state will also likely apply some type of calculation to determine what is owed. Instead of pulling out calculators, the attorneys will likely put all this information into a fancy family law computer software program, which factors in how much income both parties receive and the length of the marriage. It will then spit out an amount of money and a length of time, informing what the state guidelines are for alimony or maintenance. This may be the amount you actually use or it may be a starting point from where you negotiate. I have had clients deviate away from the guideline for maintenance—some get more and some get less, and that was accepted by both parties.

Reasons clients deviate from the statute vary. Sometimes the client may get more of a certain asset in exchange for maintenance. Other clients do a lump sum payment, while others agree to pay for 20+ years. Then there are other factors to consider, such as the clients' ages and if they seek to retire soon. Or maybe one spouse has not worked for a few years but is capable of employment—in that case, maybe it is fair to impute a certain income to that spouse.

Let your attorney know what is most important to you, and then she can help you strategize how to get there.

Dividing Assets and Debts

Assets

The assets that will be divided will include everything and the kitchen sink (well, not literally the kitchen sink, but I *have* definitely divided dishes and kitchen items). This will include checking, savings, and retirement accounts, pensions, brokerage accounts, life insurance policies, the marital residence, any other real property owned, timeshares, mobile homes, cars, boats, businesses, and lastly, all personal property items.

You will need to work through each individual account or item and determine how it will be divided: all to one spouse, a 50/50 split, or maybe a certain percentage will go to each. If you are dividing a few accounts, it may make sense to give one spouse a larger percentage of the brokerage account and the other to keep the smaller savings account already titled in that spouse's name. When working with an attorney, they can input all the information and help you look at the overall percentages each spouse will receive to help you compute fair calculations on all the assets.

In determining how to divide a business interest, it may be necessary to get a business valuation. In dividing property, it may be necessary to factor in capital gains costs if the property is sold. Again, here is where your attorney will help you.

The date of the actual marriage may create an unfair property settlement. For example, if one spouse bought property before the legal marriage date, it may be considered individual property and not considered as marital property and therefore not subject to the marital property division. Because property division is based on a judge's discretion, some may take into consideration the years of cohabitation, but there are no guarantees that you will walk away with anything your spouse purchased before your wedding. If this is something you want to make sure happens, then you may want to consider a premarital or post-nuptial agreement. See more about that below.

Debts

The parties will also need to decide how all of the debts will be divided. This is similar to dividing the assets and will be considered in connection with the overall calculation. It may not be an even split, but instead may be allocated according to who *acquired* the debt.

This gets me to a subject that is close to home: student loans. For young (or younger) couples who have "grown up" with student loans like I have, this may be a huge issue that would need to be addressed. Generally, this debt will be allocated to the spouse who acquired such debt. I have, however, mediated a matter where one spouse agreed to pay half of the other spouse's student loans until they were paid in full. This was due to the fact that the couple had a child together and without the support of the student loan payments, the other spouse knew the parent would not be able to provide for themselves and the child. That's the beauty of mediation: it gives the parties a lot of freedom to create an agreement that works for them.

Not every spouse is so generous, so don't think they all work out this way. However, it can be equitable[11] to allocate some of the student loan responsibility to the spouse receiving maintenance and benefitting from that student loan, even though that particular spouse did not attend school.

This brings us to the other big calculation that will need to be decided, which is child support.

Child Issues

Whether you are married or not, if there are children involved with a couple, there will need to be certain issues resolved in order to effectively manage the child's needs. The state will want to make sure that the child's needs are being met and, in order to do so, will look at or address certain issues.

First and foremost, child support is one of the biggest issues that will need to be addressed. The attorneys may compute the number of nights

---

[11] *Equitable* – Just; conformable to the principles of natural justice and right. Just, fair, and right, in consideration of the facts and circumstances of the individual's case. Existing in equity; available or sustainable only in equity, or only upon the rules and principles of equity. *Equitable*, Black's Law Dictionary, (2nd ed, 2021).

the child is with each parent and how much each parent makes to come up with a reasonable amount for child support. Or they may just look at the income of each parent and use percentages of that income to come up with an amount. This number can be tweaked or modified, but generally speaking, no matter how the number is derived the courts intent is to make sure the children are being cared for and that both parents are contributing to the child's needs. The support can also be affected by existing judgments, payments to additional children, and maintenance payments.

In addition to the support the child is to receive, the parents will also need to determine how the child's other expenses should be handled, such as health insurance, extra curricular activities, cell phones, cars and car insurance, and college, to name a few. This is going to depend on where and with whom the child resides.

Child Visitation & Other Things to Be Decided

There are a number of ways to create a visitation schedule. First, the parents will need to determine whose house is going to be the primary residence of the child. Couples can choose to do a true 50/50 breakdown of time, but you will still want to decide an address to list for mail, etc. Visitation schedules can vary greatly, but here are some of the most common arrangements:

- Alternating weekends and one day during the week
- The child is with Parent 1 M-F and Parent 2 on alternating weekends. They are also with Parent 2 every Wednesday (or whatever day the parents decide).
- Alternating weeks – Parent 1 has the child Sunday evening to Sunday evening. Parent 2 has the child the following week, from those times.
- Alternating every 3/4 days – The parents alternate, where one parent has the child Monday – Wednesday, the other parent has the child Thursday-Friday, and then they switch.

You will also want to determine who will have the right to be with the child on certain holidays.

Here are some of the most common holidays that are incorporated into a parenting plan:

- New Year's Eve and New Year's Day
- Easter
- Passover
- Memorial Day
- Fourth of July
- Labor Day
- Halloween
- Thanksgiving
- Friday after Thanksgiving
- Hanukkah /Christmas (and Christmas Eve)
- Birthdays – Some share it and others alternate it.

Holiday Breaks

These will consist of winter break from school, spring break, and summer break. Sometimes the parents just keep the same visitation schedule in place, but other times, they specifically state the right for one parent to take the children on vacation for the whole of spring break. Then, the other parent may have the right to do so the following year. The same works for the winter breaks. One parent may have the right to take the children for a whole week and on vacation the first week of winter break, and the other parent the second week. They may then alternate weeks every year.

Summer breaks can look very different than the regular school year visitation plan, or it may stay the same (if both parents are working or have jobs that are not adaptable). Sometimes the parents completely redo the parenting plan over summer to factor in how the children will not be in school, and also to allow for vacations.

In connection with that, the parents will also want to discuss permitted travel with the child and what information and notice shall be given to the other parent.

Extracurricular activities

In addition to determining who has the children on what day at what time, the parents will need to determine if both parents are free to go to all sports games/events and extra curricular activities during their scheduled or unscheduled times, or if it should be limited to the parent with the parenting time. You will also want to decide who is going to pay those expensive hockey fees now. I have had clients choose to split everything equally, have one parent pay for all expenses, or even have one parent pay for a certain child/expenses and the other parent pay for the other child's expenses and activities.

Health, Education, etc.

There are also the regular day-to-day parenting decisions that will need to be addressed. For example, which parent has the right to make health care and educational decisions? What if it was an emergency, and a medical decision needed to be addressed immediately? Should elective medical procedures versus emergency medical issues be addressed differently? Again, all of this will be discussed with the attorney who will help you sort out these issues.

Communication

Another fun topic that the parents will need to work out is how they wish to <u>communicate</u> with each other about the visitation sessions and everything else. Unfortunately, "not at all" is not really an option, so they'll need to determine if communication by text or email or whatever else is the best way. The parents will also need to decide how communication works with the other parent while the child is visiting the other parent. For example, does the child have the right to call the parent at all times of day or night, only certain times, or is there a scheduled communication time with the other parent?

College

Lastly, although your kiddos may be legal adults, there are some parenting issues that follow into adulthood and one of those is college. Parents may also want to consider the expense of college and each parent's contribution toward that expense.

Summary

In summary, here is a list of some of the big issues that will need to be determined in a dissolution of marriage and/or parenting agreement:

- Alimony or Maintenance
- Child Support
- Division of Assets and Debts (consisting of the house, retirement accounts, pensions, savings accounts, life insurance policies, businesses, etc.)
- Child Related Issues
    - Visitation schedule
    - Holiday schedule
    - Permitted Travel
    - Health insurance coverage
    - Extra-curricular activities (who is going to them and who is paying)
    - Communication with the child

Depending on your unique situation, there will likely be other issues to address as well. This is simply a list of some of the biggest components to decide in most divorces or parenting plans. Before you proceed with a dissolution of marriage or parenting plan though, you will need to determine the process of how your matter will be handled.

PROCEDURE

Although the issues will be the same (meaning you will still need to determine who gets what and who pays this or that), the *way* you get divorced can be totally unique. Here are some procedural options for how to handle divorce.

Traditional Divorce

Of course, this may vary a little bit depending on your state, but for the most part, the procedure of a traditional divorce goes something like this:

One party hires an attorney, who then prepares and files a petition with the court—which is "petitioning" the court for the divorce. That party (well, usually that party's attorney actually) has it served (with a sheriff or process server, depending on your state) on the other party. The other party then has a certain number of limited days to file an appearance in the matter. Now the case is on the court call and generally the parties (or their attorneys, or both) have to show up for court every 30 days or so to inform the court of the status of the divorce. The judge is there to oversee what is going on in the matter, and every time the party's or their attorney's go before the judge, the judge is making sure the case is moving along and helping it to do so. If the parties are not playing nicely, the judge may need to order one of the parties to do something (like pay child support in the interim or stop harassing the soon-to-be ex-spouse). Eventually, through this process, the parties either reach an agreement or they go to trial. Depending on the parties (and how much they want to contest every issue), the other attorneys involved, the complexity of the assets/debts, the parenting arrangements, the business complexities, and the support arrangements, the fees for a traditional divorce can cost anywhere from a few thousand dollars to millions of dollars.

Side note here: I feel like most people have heard this before, but have not really listened. I'm always surprised when clients come to me and are dismayed that their divorce cost them $50,000 and they are not even finished yet. The stories and the amounts you have heard from other people are real! I'm here to tell you, they are *real,* and many divorces are *really* expensive. In fact, a recent estimate for a typical litigated divorce for both parties is $73,550.[12] In my personal opinion, I would say that figure is probably a little low.

I say all this not to scare the daylights out of you, but so you know what you are getting into. It may still very well be worth it, but you should know and anticipate that it can be very expensive before you start.

Other Options

If you are thinking, "Holy shit balls, I better stick with my partner," that is not the point. While divorce can be expensive, sometimes it is worth it to get out of a bad situation and have a happy life. Personally, I feel like living your best life is priceless.

Also, there are other options for how to procedurally handle the divorce, which can cost a whole lot less. Two alternative methods are through Collaborative Divorce and Mediation.

The good news is, you can always try these options and, if they do not work, you can go to a traditional litigated divorce. While the cost may be a big potential benefit to doing a collaborative divorce, the *biggest* reason I like to encourage couples to at least consider a more amicable process is because of the long-term effects.

Trust me, I've met many people who have gone through nasty divorces and, years later, still have a visceral reaction whenever someone mentions divorce. It can literally suck the life out of people, and that's not even factoring in what it does to the kids.

---

[12]   Elizabeth F. Beyer, Divorce Without Court: A Guide to Mediation and Collaborative Divorce 40 St. Mary's L.J. 303, 55 (2006).

(Legal disclaimer: I'm not a scientist nor an adult/child psychologist. I'm an attorney, who has real life experience in the thick of it with families going through divorce. I have experienced very amicable divorces where the couple has literally gone to have a beer afterward to celebrate the transition, and the nastiest divorces where the couple drags each other through the mud and resembles the first scene in *Wedding Crashers*. These are just my observations and my opinions on the effects divorce has on the individuals involved.)

A few years back I attended a family legal training where they asked some very brave young adults to tell their stories of what it was like being a child when their parents were going through divorce. This training changed me and hit me hard. It made me realize just how important this moment was in some people's lives. Of these brave young individuals, one had a very traumatic experience because the divorcing parents truly hated each other. Abuse was involved in that situation. Another had parents who fought all the time, and the divorce was pretty nasty. The parents still hated each other and did not talk, did not share holidays, etc. The last one had parents who were able to effectively co-parent through and after the divorce. The ex-spouses were not best friends, but they both had new partners and were able to be civil around each other.

They all stated that it was a difficult time during the actual divorce, but what was most interesting to me was to see how these young adults were now.

As you may have guessed, the one who had experienced the most traumatic divorce (with the abuse involved) did not appear to be doing well. She didn't seem particularly happy, and her body language communicated that she was uncomfortable and meek. Her voice and demeanor signaled that she was sad. She was not in a relationship, and neither was her mother. She was not in school, nor did she have any drive to work toward making a better life for herself.

The second person was also not in school, but seemed to have a more upbeat disposition. Regardless, you could tell she still struggled to find her way. What was the most interesting, though, was that the last individual was in college and wanted to become a lawyer. That person was in a committed relationship and had a positive outlook on life. As stated, both parents had moved on and were in committed relationships, and both parents accepted the new partners of their ex-spouses.

Obviously, there can be a number of other factors playing into all their situations and where they are now, but I can't help but believe the divorce, the effects of it, and how the parents interacted with each other played a significant role.

Divorce can be grueling, mentally, physically, and emotionally. However, when the couple can proceed through it more amicably and with mutual respect, it can help minimize those negative effects so the parties (and the children) involved are better able to transition into the next stage in their lives.

Side note: I have heard other attorneys say, write, and post on social media that people should *not* try these alternative ways of dissolving marriages, and that it is better to just litigate from the start. Every person is entitled to their opinion, but in my opinion, that is complete *bullshit!*

It never hurts to *try* to resolve a conflict amicably, first. Ever. When trying to get our kids to resolve an argument, we don't tell them to go punch their friend in the face and see if that helps them get what they want, do we? Similarly, I don't suggest kicking your spouse in the gut if you actually want to get more of your possessions, money, time with your kids, respect, etc.

Traditional Divorce Summarized

To summarize, the most widely used process of handling a divorce is the traditional way. This consists of each party hiring an attorney and having those attorneys file their appearances in court on the matter. The attorneys will then receive all of the communications regarding the matter. They will navigate and lead their clients through the divorce process. They will counsel the parties and help in attaining a settlement and if that cannot be accomplished, may go to trial on behalf of their clients. After trial, the judge will make the final decision regarding who gets what.

COLLABORATIVE DIVORCE

O
f the more amicable approaches, I'm first going to discuss collaborative divorce. In a <u>Collaborative Divorce,</u> each party retains his or her own counsel, but everyone involved agrees to collaborate in the negotiation and settlement process. The parties, the attorneys, and possibly a team of therapists and/or financial advisors will work together to help the parties reach an amicable resolution.

The case is not filed with the court until the resolution is *already* reached, so the parties do not have to worry about the stress of litigation and going to trial. They do not have to worry about the unknowns of how the process will work or if it will spiral out of control. They do not have to worry about a judge telling them how often they see their kids. They also do not have to worry that they are hiring a wolf in sheep's clothing, because when the Participation Agreement is signed, it prohibits the attorneys from continuing to represent the parties if the parties decide to litigate the matter in court.

This is huge. If a Participation Agreement is not signed, well for one, it wouldn't be a "true" collaborative divorce, but really more of a "cooperative divorce" (see below for more info on cooperative divorces). In this situation, the attorney on one side can try to chirp negative, fearful thoughts in his or her client's ear and turn the amicable couple into *Avengers*-style enemies. Once it's on, it's on. And guess who stands to make a whole shit ton of money from it? You guessed it, the divorce attorneys.

But, in a *true, collaborative divorce,* that is not the case. If the attorneys convince their clients to litigate, they have to resign as the attorney, so, they lose the client! This is the big unique thing about a collaborative divorce. There is no vested interest in getting the clients to fight for unnecessary things.

If you are worried that means your attorney will not fight for you because it is collaborative, that is not true. Lawyers argue. It's what we do. We do this to get the best deal for our clients, and also because we generally like to. We've been trained at negotiating and we're usually pretty good at it. Also, a lawyer has a duty to zealously represent his or her client.

See the thing is, through the duty to "zealously represent" our clients, it allows lawyers to rationalize their part in destroying otherwise civil relationships and families by getting the client the very best they can. The problem is, this can result in getting the party to fight for an extra $100 a month in maintenance or alimony, even though it's not really worth it in the end.

Yes, there are times when fighting for just a little more isn't really worth it when you factor in *the whole picture*. For example, let's say a wife is encouraged to fight for more money in maintenance or alimony. In the short term, this sounds great, right? But what the lawyer isn't revealing is that the other attorney is not going to want to allow that to happen (obviously). The other party is then pissed that he/she has to spend a bunch of money in attorney fees to fight this now, because the other attorney "has to" fight for their client's interests, and the war is on. Both parties put up their dukes and the fight is on like Donkey Kong.

In the long run, the couple is just going to spend more of their money to fight with their lawyers. So even though one may end up getting a little more in support, in the end, the pot of money has dwindled down and there is less overall to be divided.

This can happen for various reasons. More often than not it is because the client is driving from an emotional pain point. This actually happens quite often, and it's happened to me. A client has in his or her head that they should get this certain thing for whatever reason. I, as the attorney, know the judge is not likely to give the client what she wants. I inform the client of this, but she wants to fight for it anyway. Now I am essentially wasting both parties' money to keep fighting for an issue I know is a bunch of baloney. In the end, the parties just spent down their assets, no party was any better off (now they just hate each other even more), and the attorneys made a bunch of money.

Don't get me wrong—it's not that this cannot happen in a collaborative divorce, but it is less likely in that the client knows if they keep pushing for unrealistic demands, the whole collaborative process is going to implode. The matter will then go into litigation, both parties will lose their current attorneys and have to find new representation, and it will be all that person's fault.

Again, in a collaborative divorce, the attorney is still going to fight to get child support, but they are not going to encourage *unrealistic expectations*. That would only cause the parties to fight more, likely fall out of the collaborative process, and go to trial, which means both attorneys lose. Do you see why this works?

There is one caveat: sometimes, a client or a party just wants to fight to fight. Trust me, I totally get it. During the COVID-19 quarantine, I was an inch away from filing a petition against my Vrbo rental after they wouldn't let me cancel my trip despite being in a flipping global pandemic! I was about to spend way more money in billable hours to rip this guy a new one and make his life hell, then the thousand dollars I was about to lose. At that time, I truly did not care and welcomed it. My husband had to talk me off the proverbial ledge. I had to question myself if it was really going to make my life better in the end.

I didn't end up filing the lawsuit and we came to an agreement, but my point is, I get it. If my husband cheated on me with the secretary, I would want to cut his balls off too (love you honey)! But the truth is, the only person unrealistic demands are going to end up hurting is the person starting the fight. Well, maybe the other party too, but really in the end they will both end up spending all their combined money and neither will get the sense of peace and happiness they are desiring.

Now trust me, sometimes litigation is necessary. When that is the case, it makes sense to have an awesome litigation attorney. The couple I am suggesting should consider a collaborative divorce is not the couple who should get a litigation attorney from the outset.

The couple who should consider a collaborative divorce

In my experience, I would say a collaborative divorce works for the couple who can be reasonable despite being hurt, angry, or sad. They can and are willing to put their emotions aside for their benefit. Again, it's not for everyone, but when used by the couple that is able to do this, collaborative divorce can offer a really nice alternative way to handle the process. A good percentage of my clients do it for privacy reasons as they do not want anything leaked about their personal affairs to the public. Others are business owners who, again, want everything to remain private so it does not affect their reputation and business.

If you are considering a collaborative divorce, the most important part is to make sure you hire a true collaborative attorney. Be careful of attorneys who claim to be collaborative but are actually strong litigation firms with an occasional collaborative divorce. There may be some firms out there who may prove this statement wrong, but by and large, my experience has been that firms that mostly do litigation have a litigation mind set. My advice is, don't go into shark-infested waters hoping to see a dolphin. Instead, hire a collaboratively trained and certified divorce attorney whose practice consists mostly of collaborative divorce or other forms of alternative dispute resolutions, as mentioned below.

Cooperative Divorce

A cooperative divorce is somewhat of a hybrid of a traditional divorce and a collaborative divorce. The big difference in a cooperative divorce is that there is not (usually) a Participation Agreement (which states that the parties will not file a petition to start a lawsuit) in the court until a resolution has been reached wherein, if it turns into litigation, the attorneys cannot represent the parties. Therefore, in this style, the attorneys *may* still have the ability to go in and represent their client through litigation.

Side note: I have signed a hybrid of the Collaborative Participation Agreement which was morphed for the cooperative practice. It had the same general intent as the Collaborative Participation Agreement, but without the places for the financial advisors or therapists to sign. It also didn't force the attorneys to recuse themselves from the matter in the event that it went to trial, but, it did state that the parties and the attorneys are all agreeing that they will try their best to work cooperatively together to reach a resolution. I actually really liked this Cooperative Participation Agreement, and the matter went very smoothly. In my opinion it's okay to be creative in this process. To me, the biggest factor is figuring out what is going to work for the parties.

Not all cooperative divorces are the same. Because a cooperative divorce is a hybrid of a traditional divorce and a collaborative, they can be more lopsided one way or the other. Sometimes the Maltipoo looks like a Maltese but doesn't shed like a poodle, or sometimes it looks like a poodle but has the personality of a Maltese. Essentially, they are not all the same. So, it's important to voice what you want to your lawyer and make clear the type of representation you would like. The lawyer should inform you of what you're up against (meaning, how the other attorney carries on and also the jurisdiction).

Side note: I absolutely love when Elle Woods uses the term "subject matter jurisdiction" to sound smart and help get her friend's dog back in *Legally Blonde*. But, in reality, jurisdiction just refers to the power of the court to hear the case. In this case, I'm using it to reference that the location of the court where you file will have an impact on your matter. That is because all cities, states, and counties have their own laws and policies they follow. Some jurisdictions are more progressive and some are more conservative. For that matter, so are the judges! It's kind of like when dealing with teachers in school or bosses at work—you never really know what you're going to get. They all have guidelines to follow, but can be subjective in how they apply them. Your lawyer will tell you what you're in for, so you know what to expect ahead of time. This will likely determine what your cooperative divorce looks like.

Okay, back to cooperative divorce. As long as the attorney on the other side is also willing to do the same, then even though the paperwork is filed in court, it can still be very amicable. It can also be fast and inexpensive. Again, the biggest matter of concern here is not to hire a wolf in sheep's clothing. This is usually apparent right away when you look at the petition. If the petition was supposed to be a 50/50 shared parenting agreement but instead is asking for full custody, *be careful!* You know the old saying: if it looks like a duck and quacks like a duck, it's probably a duck.

That is not always the case, though. A cooperative divorce can also look just like a collaborative divorce, but may involve one attorney who is not collaboratively trained. This attorney agrees to play nice and not file anything with the court until the agreements have been reached. Again, this can be very amicable, fast, and inexpensive.

Personally, I like and do a lot of cooperative divorces. I'm willing to work with what comes to me, even if it's not a true collaborative divorce. As long as the other attorney is willing to be fair and not pull any sneaky moves, I'm fine with it for my client. It *is* more risky, though, and I have definitely had the other attorney then file and ask for a pretrial conference right away (a conference before a matter goes to trial where the judge gives his or her opinion on the matter). This can actually be a good settlement tactic in a traditional divorce, but it sort of defeats the purpose of doing an amicable divorce where the parties should have all of the power.

Summary

In summary, a collaborative divorce is where the parties agree to collaborate together with their attorneys, and other professionals as needed, to work towards and reach a settlement. Upon reaching a settlement, the attorneys will then draft the agreements, present them, and get them entered by the court to finalize everything.

Okay, enough about collaborative and cooperative divorces. Now onto my personal fave.

MEDIATION

Consider the value of a trustworthy, experienced mediator who has the ability to isolate difficult issues and help people work collaboratively and without animosity toward a successful conclusion. Through using the mediation process, the couple agrees to try to keep the matter outside of court. The process consists of the parties working with a neutral third party to help settle and reach an agreement on all the issues that go into the divorce or child care agreement. This can include maintenance, support, custody, and division of assets and debts.

In my mediation practice, I carefully listen to what each party wants and ensure each party feels heard. I try to be creative and don't have a one-size-fits-all mediation approach. Instead, I work with clients to help them get to a resolution by using a combination of face-to-face meetings, phone calls, electronic communication via Zoom or FaceTime, and private caucuses to help reach a settlement. Sometimes I use all joint meetings, and occasionally there are times I never put the parties together. I had one particular mediation where one party stated he would end the mediation if he was ever put in the same room with his wife. For that mediation, I assured him I was not going to trick him. I never put them in the same room together or even had them come in to meet with me around the same times. It worked, and they were able to work out a successful agreement. In essence, I tailor the mediations to fit the parties' needs so I can help them get to a settlement.

Mediation is a powerful tool to move forward, as it gives both parties the ability to control issues and outcomes that are best for each individual and the family unit.

I love mediation, because the parties have the *most* control. Essentially, because there are fewer cooks in the kitchen, it can be the fastest and most efficient divorce method. That doesn't mean that it is *always* the best choice, but I can say that in most of my mediations we come to an agreement faster than in the other alternative ways aforementioned.

In mediation, the mediator is facilitating the negotiation but it is the parties, not the attorneys, working directly with the mediator. This gives the parties more control and flexibility over their cases and ensure their feelings and desires are heard. Unlike a traditional or collaborative divorce case, the mediator cannot represent one party over another. Instead, the mediator acts as a neutral third party to help the *parties* reach a settlement agreement. The mediator will not go to court to represent either party. The mediator may also work with a team of professionals, like in a collaborative divorce, to reach a resolution.

My personal style is mostly facilitative, meaning I help the parties sort out the details of their own agreement. We collaboratively find real solutions without any judgment. Importantly, all the information shared is confidential and out of the sight of a public court; the parties are free to negotiate an agreement that feels right to them. Finally, mediation genuinely improves future communication with a former spouse, which makes issues down the road far easier to resolve.

Why is this Different?

The biggest difference in mediation is that the mediator is *not advising* the parties. He or she will not encourage one party to fight harder and ask for more, like an attorney would. The attorney's job is to look for ways to get the *best* deal for their client, as explained above, while in mediation, the mediator is simply trying to help the parties come to an agreement they both feel comfortable with. Some mediators take an *evaluative approach,* which is when the mediator may evaluate the matter and give their opinions to help facilitate the agreement. Many attorneys and judges are mediators, so they can easily step in and warn the parties if something is not likely to be approved by the judge or fall too far outside the scope of approved guidelines.

Some mediators are not attorneys and will not take an evaluative approach. These mediators will only stick with a facilitative approach, meaning they are only there to help facilitate the mediation and are not going to evaluate it. This is something you may want to ask your mediator about to see what style they use.

Either way, the mediator will work through some or all of the issues to help the parties create a parenting plan and/or achieve a dissolution of marriage (divorce).

Sometimes the parties may be each working with attorneys and proceeding through a traditional divorce, when the judge orders the parties to mediation to help resolve a particular pain point. This can be really useful and a great way to get the parties to reach a resolution and avoid trial over one little issue.

Attorneys are sometimes used in the mediation process, and sometimes the mediators prefer for the attorneys not to be involved. Sometimes the attorneys just help afterward, to help draft the paperwork for the clients after they have reached a settlement. They will then prepare and file the paperwork with the court to finalize the matter.

In summary, a mediation, at minimum involves the two parties and the mediator. It may also include attorneys, children, and other professionals. The mediator is not representing or advocating for one party over another. Instead, the mediator is a neutral third person working with and openly communicating with the parties to help them achieve an agreement.

Overview

Here is an overview of the alternative methods of divorce and parentage issues.

Whether a client is doing a collaborative divorce, cooperative divorce, or mediation, some of the benefits and differences from a traditional divorce are:

1. <u>Each Parties' Voice is Heard</u>. Each party has the ability to openly voice their wants and concerns. This allows for creating agreements that adhere to both parties' needs and avoids a one-sided judgment.

2. The Emotional Well-Being of the Parties is Better Off. The parties are generally better able to cope and move on when they were a part of the process and helped create the resolution and agreement they are going to live by. This passes onto the little ones, too. As we all know, the littles pick up on our energy and attitudes. If Mom and Dad feel content with the agreement they helped create, the kids will have a greater acceptance and peace with it.

3. Financially Less Burdensome. On average, couples spend less when proceeding through a collaborative or cooperative process, than they do with a litigated one. That translates to more money for each party to live off of once the divorce is final, and that can also bring greater peace of mind. Again, this passes onto the little ones. I'm only *touching* on the impact the financial aspect of divorce can have on the parties and the children, but I realize that this can actually be a very big issue to many people considering this process for divorce. That being said, I strongly suggest that it is not the only driving factor in considering these alternative processes. I can almost always tell when couples actually want to fight and are just trying to use a collaborative process to spend less money. This just wastes everyone's time, as the matter eventually turns litigated anyway.

4. Confidentiality and Privacy. Through attorney-client confidentiality, the parties do not have to worry about airing their dirty laundry to the public. Even if the parties decide to litigate later, the negotiations during the mediation will still be confidential and the mediator cannot be subpoenaed to testify. This gives the parties the ability to have faith and trust in the process. This is also a big factor to many clients for a variety of reasons. Some people have businesses and do not want certain things to come up during the divorce that could potentially hurt the owners or the reputation of the business.

5. Free from litigation. When handling a divorce in an amicable way, you don't have to worry about a sheriff showing up at your door or any of the other scary unknowns that happen during litigation.

6. Promotes Communication and Cooperation. This can be especially important if you have to continue to co-parent for many years.

7. <u>Parties Have the Most Control.</u> The parties are captains steering the ship and the professionals are helping them get there.
8. <u>Not Uncontested!</u> Although the name may give that impression, unfortunately, a collaborative divorce does not mean it is uncontested and the parties agree on everything. Instead, it refers to *the process* of how the couples reach a resolution.

Whether you are doing a collaborative divorce, cooperative divorce, or mediation, it is a step toward settling your dispute amicably. The more contentious the divorce becomes, the more emotionally distressing it is on each party. This is especially so considering the close bond the parties once had. In addition, children can particularly have a difficult time in dealing with divorce, because their whole world is changing and they don't have a say in it. The parties staying amicable and cooperative shows the children that the parents still respect and care for each other, which may help them accept the situation better. Also, what a great lesson to teach the kids.

The best compliments I get are when clients reach out to me after the divorce and thank me for helping them. It is gratifying to see that, because of the process we used, the clients (and their children) are able to move on to the next chapter in their lives.

Divorces and Parenting Issues In General

Unfortunately, the amicable process is not a right fit for everyone and sometimes litigation is necessary or the best option. If you find yourself in a situation where you are heading for a divorce or need to determine child support and other related parenting issues, it is best to meet with a professional to help guide you. The professional should be able to assess and determine which process is the best fit for your situation and guide you down that path.

PART IV
MOVIN' ON UP

Attorneys and legal services are not only needed for the bad times, but can be important in the good times as well. Whether that means getting married, buying a house, or starting a new business, there are benefits to meeting with your attorney as you go into the new venture.

TYING THE KNOT

S orry to be a buzzkill, but the dream of being a blushing bride one day and raising kids in a happily ever after is not always how it works out. Because of that, I want to give a strong shout out to premarital agreements (also called prenuptial agreements, or "prenups") and post-marital agreements.

A premarital agreement is an agreement you created before the marriage began, stating that if things do not work out, this is how the assets will be divided. A post-marital agreement can essentially state the same thing, but it is an agreement created after the marriage has already begun.

Who should use these?

1. People with a lot of money (obviously). This doesn't have to mean Rockefeller-type money, but enough money that it will really suck if your ex-spouse takes half of it.
2. People who will inherit a lot of money.
3. The other spouse has a lot of debt.
4. Second or more marriages, where there is already a large payout to kids or spouses of prior marriages.
5. People who own a business.
6. People with properties and separate assets they want to maintain and keep as separate.
7. People who want to protect their assets in case of a dissolution of marriage.

8. People who have been through nasty divorces (either themselves, or parents, etc.) and want the dissolution of the marriage process to be smoother.

If you are unsure whether or not a premarital or post-marital agreement is a good idea for you, reach out to a local attorney and he/she will let you know. Premarital/post-marital agreements range in complexity (depending on the client's needs) and cost. Some are relatively simple and inexpensive to create, so it's better to be safe than sorry. Others, as you may imagine, can be very complex, detailed, and cost a good chunk of change—but in those cases, it's a no brainer that it's worth it. To make it more complicated, the laws of what is acceptable in each state vary. Many states have adopted the Uniform Premarital Agreement Act, which lays out the framework for what is required to have an effective premarital agreement.

Why are they so awesome?

What's nice is that a premarital/post-marital agreement will state how the estates will be divided in the event of a divorce *or* death. Yes, you read that right. There is crossover into the estate planning stuff I mentioned earlier. Not only does it help create a less complicated divorce in the event the parties decide to separate, but it can also make estate administration easier if one spouse passes away.

For example, let's say Wife remarries but wants to make it so that if she passes, all of her money goes into a trust for the benefit of her children from her first marriage. It would be important for her premarital or post-marital agreement with her second husband to state that, to show the court that it was agreed upon by the parties. That way, if her second spouse comes in after her death and tries to ask for more through a spousal election, he would be out of luck.

Again, depending on your jurisdiction, the premarital/post-marital agreement will vary as to what can go into it and the requirements needed to make it valid. Most family law attorneys also do premarital and post-marital agreements, so the first place to start is to contact a local family law attorney. Let them know what it is you want to protect, and they can inform you of what is allowed/not allowed for your jurisdiction.

Summary

In summary, if you have built up a little nest egg for yourself, you should consider protecting it before entering into a marriage. If you're already married, you may be able to do a post marital agreement to protect those assets, but that will be dependent upon the state that you reside in.

BUYING YOUR DREAM HOME... OR STARTER HOME

In some states they don't use attorneys in residential real estate trans-actions—however in other states, they do. I'm going to talk a little bit about it here in the event that you are purchasing your first home (or maybe an investment property) and you're wondering if you should use an attorney.

After the contract is signed—meaning, after you find your dream house, you put in an offer, and the buyer accepts—it feels like party time! Well, I'm sorry to tell you, the contract is actually not set in stone yet. There is a period of time which is called the "attorney review period" where the attorneys (meaning the buyers' attorney and the sellers' attorney) will still continue to negotiate the contract terms the agreement is based on. Sometimes the modifications to the contract are minor, yet other times, they are quite extensive. Both attorneys are trying to get the most and protect their respective party's interests.

For example, the sellers' attorney might ask for a home warranty. This would be so that, in the event that something in the house, like a refrigerator, later malfunctions or in the first year that the buyer owns the house, has a means to have that appliance fixed or replaced. Maybe that was something the real estate brokers never discussed but, after speaking with your real estate attorney, you realize it's something that you would really like. In that case, the buyers' attorney would ask for a home warranty for the property, which may cost the seller around $500 (though, a request doesn't mean the sellers' attorney is going to agree).

That is just an example of one type of modification. There are a whole list of issues the buyers' attorney and seller's attorney will discuss. A more important issue that may be negotiated is something like radon testing if the property is located in an area that is known for having high levels of radon. In that case, the buyers' attorney may request that there be a test to see what the current levels are and, if that test does not meet a certain standard, then the sellers will take any actions necessary to get the levels to an agreeable level.

Also, usually sometime in this attorney review period, the house will be inspected. The attorneys generally want this to fall within the attorney review period so that if there are any issues with the house, the attorneys can negotiate how the seller will correct or mitigate the damages for the buyers.

If you are buying a condo, townhouse, or property in an area where there is a Homeowner's Association (HOA), the documents controlling the association—showing what they have in reserves, minutes from the board meetings, etc.—will also need to be ordered. If it is found, the Association does not have enough in reserves or if they seem a little sketchy, this could make or break a deal. HOAs can be difficult to deal with, but it is important to know who you are getting involved with before doing so.

As an example, I once had a client who sadly had to deal with a truly awful HOA. This HOA hated my client so much that they tried everything in their power to block them from selling their property. They would do silly things to get potential buyers to back out of the deal. It's ironic, actually, as you would think the HOA would want the sellers to leave and make it easy for them to do so. Luckily (for my sellers), in the end, the sale still went through. Not sure how those buyers currently feel about their HOA, though.

I personally find, as an attorney who has done real estate, that a good chunk of my work is done during this attorney review period. This is where you are really getting the best bang for your buck and the attorney is earning his/her money.

Once the attorney review period is over, there are usually a couple weeks in between where the mortgage broker is working on their part to get the funding to purchase the property. During this time, the real estate agents or brokers are watching over and keeping open the lines of communications with everyone involved. They are monitoring the transactions and potentially reaching out to their respective clients on any issues that come up.

The attorneys will also work with the title company. The title company's role is to review the chain of title on the property. The chain of title is the history of all of the people that have owned or had an interest in the property or that particular piece of land. The attorneys will review the title with the title company to make sure that the person or people whom you believe you are purchasing the land from are the people who actually own the property. They are also making sure no one else has a claim on the property, like an old contractor who never got paid. Essentially, they are verifying that the sellers have the right to sell the property to the buyers.

Sometimes there are kinks in the chain of title, which the title company and the attorneys work through. This means doing some research and figuring out if that interest is going to cause an issue. The title company's role is to ensure that the title on the property is "good." So, if they find there is a lien on the property which has never been satisfied, they may need that issue fixed.

Or, maybe there is just the first mortgage recorded on the property. This is common. The title company is going to insure the property is good, that the lien on the property will go away at the time of closing, and that the bank is paid off. This will not be an issue, because that mortgage is going to be paid off at the closing with the sale of the property.

During all this time, the mortgage broker and company are working with the buyer to make sure they have everything they need in order to get the loan approved. This may require a whole bunch of paperwork you did not anticipate, which may include tax returns, W2s, bank statements, etc. Once the bank finally approves the loan, they will issue a "clear to close." This is the magic wording for all of those involved in the real estate transactions, as now the attorneys can actually schedule the closing. (Note: do not be alarmed if your closing date gets pushed back a day or two. This is common when dealing with so many variables that must be completed before scheduling the official closing date).

Once we have the closing date, the buyer will want to make sure all the work that was agreed upon to be done to the house has actually been completed. This can also be where issues come up—maybe the handyman (AKA the sellers' Uncle Louie) they hired to fix all the plumbing work is not up to the buyers' standard. In that case, there may be a little more negotiating needed to figure out whether or not the buyers or the sellers are willing to go in and fix it again. Maybe the sellers will decide to give the buyers a credit to fix the damage on their own.

Within a day or so of the scheduled closing, a closing statement will be prepared by the title company. This will show a list of all of the fees and expenses on both the sellers' side and the buyers' side. In Illinois, we actually pay our property taxes a year behind, so the sellers will give the buyers a credit for the buyers to pay the sellers' property taxes from the prior year. This is just one example of the fees that will be included in that final closing statement. It will also include your attorney's fees, your real estate transfer fees, paying off the mortgage, and any credits that are due.

Don't be surprised if this is not the number you thought it would be! There are always going to be extra closing fees you did not anticipate. It's like when you look at your cell phone bill and see a list of unexpected fees such as a "talking on the phone" fee, a service fee, the tax for having a tax fee, etc. This may be an over-exaggeration, but just know there will likely be some extra taxes and fees you did not anticipate from the city, state, and title company. The general rule of thumb is that the sellers are going to pay about 10 percent of the sale price in closing costs. Now remember, in Illinois that includes factoring in the taxes from the year before. The buyers, on average, pay about 3 percent of the sale price in closing fees.

At the closing, be prepared to sign a bunch of documents. The documents are extensive, and there are a lot of them. It can be overwhelming, but I always say to my clients, "Here's the thing: if you don't sign these, you're not getting the house today."

It is common for attorneys to sign these documents for their clients. The buyers may be there with their attorney or have a Durable Power of Attorney (DPA, see chapter 6) where the attorney is signing for them (and likewise with the sellers). It is also common for the sellers' attorney to have met with the sellers before the closing and to have had them sign most of the documents already. Then, the sellers' attorney just brings the signed documents to the closing. Those documents consist of a deed transferring the title and a Bill of Sale, among others. The deed transfers the land (usually a Warranty Deed), and the Bill of Sale gives the buildings, fixtures, and personal property on the land to the buyers.

Once all the documents are signed by both parties, the title company will submit the documents to the bank. Once the bank has funded the loan, the transaction will be complete. Now the sellers will give the buyers the keys and the garage door openers, and the buyers are free to move into their new house!

Summary

To conclude, here are some of the roles and duties of the attorney in a real estate closing:

- Draft and/or review contracts
- Check legal descriptions
- Review land surveys
- Work with the title company on the title history associated with the property
- Negotiate terms
- Review final amounts to close

As mentioned, not every state uses attorneys in real estate closings, so some of the actions listed may be performed by real estate brokers, lenders, or title companies themselves. Now, onto what I consider to be the best legal action.

ADOPTIONS

Adoptions hold the very best courtrooms in the courthouse. I particularly love the adoption court in Cook County, Illinois, because they give the child being adopted a lollipop—and sometimes a *teddy bear!* I mean, how flipping cute is that?

(Sidenote, they even give these gifts to adult adoptions, as well. This acknowledges the little kid in all of us.)

Unlike some other courtrooms, these courtrooms are not meant to be scary. In my experience, the judges are totally understanding and sympathetic to the adopting parents and to the children being adopted. They realize that court can be intimidating for many people and they do their best to make it a good experience.

Adopting a child is a bit of a process, though—and I'm not even talking about the process of finding the right child to adopt (that's for another book).

Once you have found the child who is meant to become a part of your family, you must prove to the court that you are worthy of adopting the child. In order to do this, the court will want to investigate you and your living situation to make sure it is appropriate, safe, and in the best interests of the child.

To do this, the court will appoint a Guardian ad Litem (GAL). These people are known as "the eyes and the ears of the court." GALs are also referenced in adult and minor guardianships, and may also be involved in disputed child visitation issues. A GAL will be tasked with interviewing the adopting parents, meeting with the children to be adopted, and reaching out to other people known to and by the children. These people can include close relatives, teachers, caretakers, friends, etc. They may also visit where the child will be living and ensure the child has a clean and safe place to sleep. After interviewing the child and family, the GAL will write a report for the judge assessing the child's situation.

Again, a GAL is not someone to be feared. All the GALs I know do it because they genuinely care and want the best for the parties involved. They are people too, and they put themselves in a vulnerable and tough position to help children. It is a huge responsibility, and they take it very seriously.

Have you realized the theme I keep repeating? The *best interests of the child*. This is the standard by which all judgements regarding children are made. Therefore, if you are nervous about being rejected as the adoptive parent and about what the GAL is going to say to the judge, ask yourself: is it in the best interests of the child? There is some room for discretion and this can be a gray area, but by and large, if you use logic and trust your gut, you will know whether or not the parental action is one within the child's best interest.

For example, I pick up my child after school every day, then we eat and do homework before bed, which is at a reasonable time every night. Those would all be actions that are in the best interests of the child. Conversely, if you barely have time to clean or care for the child, the house is dirty, there is hardly enough food in the house, and the child misses school frequently, that placement might not be in the best interests of the child.

I say all of this not to scare you but to emphasize that GALs are just real people and there to write an objective assessment of the situation for the court. They just want to make sure that if the court allows the adoption to proceed, it is a wise decision.

After the GAL is finished interviewing the various people and assessing the situation, he or she will then prepare a report that is used by the court to determine if the placement is in the best interests of the child. A judge does not *have* to take the recommendation of the GAL, but they often do.

If the biological parents consent to the adoption, they will need to inform the court of this and may need to come to court to testify that they agree to it. Both parents will need to be informed and consent, even if one is incarcerated and will be for many years to come.

The judge will want to meet the children and the adopting parents to ask them a few questions and assess the situation. The judge will read the GAL's report, and maybe ask the attorney representing the parents some questions. The judge will then question the biological parents, make a determination, and then (if appropriate) order the adoption.

If it is uncontested, meaning the biological parents do not object and are easily available and able to testify to that, the whole process can take just a few months. Of course, if it *is* contested, that's going to complicate and lengthen the process.

Summary

In conclusion, when you find the child that is meant to be a part of your family, you can hire an attorney who will file and prepare all of the paperwork, work with the GAL, and help to get you appointed as the parent.

YOUR DREAM SUGARLESS, FAT-FREE, GLUTEN-FREE, COOKIE SHOP

L et's say you have been dying to start your own dream vegan, sugarless, fat-free, and gluten-free cookie shop for the last five years. You have finally saved up a little dough to do it and have the guts to jump in, but you still want to make sure you do it smart. What do I mean by being *smart* about it? I mean, "don't rush into it and hope for the best." Instead, lay down the proper foundation first so when shit hits the fan (and it always does at some point), you won't panic.

There are many reasons to own your own business, and I personally love owning mine. It took me many years to have the guts to start it, but since I did, it's been one of the best decisions I have ever made. Some advantages to having your own business include tax advantages, the ability to create and live your vision, the ability to be your own boss; and the ability to give back and employ others in your community.

But, before you even get your business off the ground, make sure the foundation of your business is solid. Depending on the business books you read, you may get advice on sales, marketing, HR, and creating policies and procedures, just to name a few. And you will likely want to (and *need* to) read these before you have the courage and basic fundamentals needed to own a business. Trust me, I've read hundreds of business books which were invaluable to me getting my business off the ground.

Or, maybe you are more of a "just jump in and do it" kind of person who sees reading all those books as just an extra hurdle for you to overcome. You would rather jump in and do it, so you don't lose your *cojones*. Either way, what I'm about to discuss here are the things you *do not want* to skip! This is the right way to protect yourself and your family so your dream cookie shop does not become a nightmare when someone accidentally chips a tooth on that nut-free cookie.

First, you need to decide what type of business you want to create. There are many types to choose from, such as a sole proprietorship, a partnership, a limited partnership, a Limited Liability Company, an S Corp, a C Corp, and a non-profit. I am going to start with the simplest (in my opinion), but also the hardest to run: the sole proprietorship.

Sole Proprietorships

The simplest way to start a business is through a sole proprietorship. This really just means you work for yourself and are self-employed. This is a legitimate business and usually involves obtaining a license to do your business, a permit, and possibly some other regulatory requirements depending on your state or city (and the type of business you are opening). You will want and need to obtain these before you start working through your business.

Uno

Sole proprietorships consist of one owner, hence the *"sole"* in "sole proprietorship." Even though you are doing business as the sole owner, you may want a fancier name, like "Cindy's Calorie-Free Cookies." In that case, you may decide to create what is called a "Doing Business As," or a "DBA," which then allows Cindy to go to the local farmer's markets and sell cookies under that name.

The Good and the Bad

If you wish to take out a loan for your cookie venture, just know that you, personally, will be solely responsible for this debt. One hundred percent responsible, in fact. So, if it ends up people don't like calorie-free cookies and you took out a loan from the bank for $10,000 to buy the equipment and ingredients, the bank can go after your personal bank accounts, equity in your house, your car, or other assets that could potentially be sold to pay back the bank.

Uno Mas

On the flip side, if it ends up people love your calorie-free cookies and can't get enough of them, your *sole* bank account will be the one filling up with cash, and you won't have to pay any other owners a share! *Cha-ching.*

Taxes

Another benefit as a sole proprietor is that you will report your profits and losses on your individual tax returns. The profits are taxed at the individual income tax rate. This is called *pass-through* taxation because it passes from the business to the individual tax return. It's nice and often preferred, because it's relatively easy to report and pay taxes on your business this way. Another thing you will want to be aware of is that you will also be solely responsible for paying for Social Security and Medicare taxes. These are called "self-employment taxes." When you work for a company, the company pays half of these taxes for you. When you work for yourself, you must pay all of it. Don't be turned off by this though—the United States is a capitalist country, and this country generally wants businesses to succeed!

Want proof of that? Currently, with the Small Business Deduction, small business owners get to take an automatic deduction of 20 percent off of their profits and do not have to pay taxes on it! This means that a business owner can reduce their taxable income. This particular deduction applies not only to sole proprietorships, but also partnerships, S Corps, and LLCs. It does not apply to C Corps (think really big corporations—like,

Wall Street big). There are also other benefits to owning your own business, such as writing off all of the business expenses before distributing the profits to the owner (you). So, if you are using your cell phone in your business, you can write a portion of it off. If you are using your car to deliver your cookies, you may be able to write a portion of it off. The moral of the story is, although you will have to pay some self-employment taxes (and you should be prepared for that when you have your own business), there are a lot of tax benefits to having your own business, as well. In the end, it can actually help you pay a lot less money to the government and put a lot more in your pockets.

So, to summarize sole proprietorships, they are super simple to create, you get to make all of the decisions, your booty is the one personally on the line for business debts, and lastly, you get to use pass-through tax treatment for your tax returns.

Partnerships

Another option you may want to consider is *not* going it alone. Maybe your bestie and you decide to open up that amazing cookie shop together. A partnership is simply two or more people holding themselves out as partners in a business for profit. Partnerships can be general or limited. First, I am going to explain a <u>General Partnership</u>.

In a General Partnership, both partners are fully liable for all profits and losses. They are both able to fully control the business. Technically, you can have as many partners in the business as you would like, but, you will have to come to an agreement with all of those people on every decision! That is, unless your Partnership Agreement states otherwise. For example, maybe one partner is the one who funded the business with his or her money, but the other partner funded the partnership with her sweat equity—meaning she will be the one running the day-to-day operations of the business. Though the partners' contributions were different, they will both be liable for the debts and will equally share in the profits.

This leads me to the importance of creating an agreement.

Partnership Agreements

This is *sooo* important. Please, *please* formalize your agreement by consulting with and having your attorney draft up a Partnership Agreement. This will lay the groundwork for how you will divide the profits and losses the partnership draws (or a payment, in lieu of a salary), how you may later sell the partnership, or what happens in the event one of you passes away. It's important to meet with an attorney, because each state may have its own specific laws in regards to how the agreement is governed.

Side note: I highly recommend partnerships! I have one, but it took me years to get over all the horror stories and actually jump into it. Now that I am in one, I love it and would do it again in a heartbeat. The biggest warning I want to give, though, is to make sure you find the *right* partner. It will need to be someone you trust, work well with, can disagree with, have respect for, and vice versa. It does NOT have to be your best friend, and honestly maybe it shouldn't be. You may put a lot more hours into your business than you originally thought, and when you leave it, it's nice to get outside advice and perspectives from someone not directly involved in it.

Also, make sure you are able to comfortably disagree with your partner. In the beginning everything may be gravy but there will come a place and time when you will have different opinions. In those times, make sure it's someone you can have an adult disagreement with. By "adult," I mean you should find someone who will not take disagreements personally or act out. Instead, you can each listen to the other's viewpoint and consider it genuinely. All that to say, although I'm forewarning you of the potential of a break-up of the business ahead of time, I actually really do love partnerships. I am also a proponent of getting married, but I strongly believe in doing a premarital agreement as well!

I believe, when you both go into an agreement with a clear understanding of what you plan to give and carefully negotiate the terms to get out, it gives more respect to the relationship and the agreement. Also, in the event you *do* want to get out of it, you will be so happy you did this beforehand.

Limited Partnerships

As the name implies, in a limited partnership, the interests are *limited*. This can be a good thing for limiting liability. For example, let's stick with the cookie business. You love your friend's cookies, but don't actually know anything about baking or running a business. When she's looking for ways to start her cookie shop, you want to invest in her, but didn't realize that was actually an option! Well, yes, it is—and your friend will be very happy I'm telling you this! You could invest in her business as a "limited partner," wherein you may not have any control of the day-to-day operations or ability to make decisions for the company, but you do own a share and receive a percentage of its profits every month. The catch is, as long as the limited partner does not participate in the management, his or her liability will stay limited. If they cross over and start making decisions on how to run the business, this shield of liability goes away.

Taxes

A partnership will be treated as a pass-through entity, like the sole proprietorship. The partnership will need to report how much each partner earned, and then each partner will need to report his or her income on a separate form that will be filed with their individual return.

Most of the time, limited partnerships will be treated like general partnerships and each of the partners will individually report and pay taxes on their share of the profits. So, if the general partner received $50,000 from the partnership and the limited partner only received $10,000 from the partnership, they will each pay an amount based on their own individual tax rate.

Unfortunately, you will still need to pay those damn same self-employment taxes like you did in the sole proprietorship, so be forewarned. The limited partners, however, do not have to pay the self-employment tax, as they are not *active* in the business.

To summarize, a partnership consists of at least two people carrying on a business together. Partnerships can be limited or general, which refers to the amount of power and liability associated with each partner. Similarly, they can also be equal where everything is split 50/50 or can have unequal distributions of profits and losses. This is dependent on what the partners agree to and then what should ultimately be stated in their Partnership Agreement.

Corporations

Corporations are a little more complicated, and each is governed by the state in which they are filed. Therefore, some of these terms may vary depending on the state in which you are planning to incorporate.

First you have the **incorporators**, who do all the prep work and the biggest job of filing the articles of incorporation with the state.

Then there are the **shareholders**, who own the stock in the corporation. An S Corp can have one stockholder owning 100 percent of the stock in the corporation. The shareholders role is to:

- Elect and remove directors
- Amend the bylaws
- Approve the sale of assets
- Approve of mergers and acquisitions
- Amend the articles of incorporation
- Dissolve the corporation

The **Directors** manage the corporation and make policy decisions. The number of directors needed may be based on the number of shareholders.

The **Officers** will run the day-to-day operations. Generally, these consist of at least the following: President (or chief operating officer), Secretary (in charge of corporate records), and Treasurer (in charge of finances).

Lastly, there are the **Employees**. These are the people who receive W2 income. In a small corporation, the shareholders may also be the employees. If you are the president, sole shareholder, and solo employee, you will hopefully receive both the W2 income *and* profit from the corporation. You will need to pay employment taxes for the employee, but then you can deduct all the business expenses before distributing a profit. The profit will be taxed at the appropriate corporate tax rate.

If you decide you want to create a corporation, you will need to prepare and file the articles of incorporation, select the board of directors, adopt bylaws, elect officers, issue stock, and lastly, decide the tax election. It always ends with taxes. *Sigh.*

In summary, a corporation is a different type of structure whereby there are shareholders, officers, and directors named to run the corporation. Each position has its role in the company and in a small corporation, one person may literally be the sole person appointed for all of them.

LLCs

Another way to structure your business is through a Limited Liability Company, (LLC). As the name implies, *it limits your liability*, which means if the LLC gets sued, they cannot go after your assets personally. *Winner winner, chicken dinner!* This is a good thing for you as a business owner. In the event someone gets sick off a cookie, they will be limited to only the assets of the business, not your personal savings account. I'm going to spend a bit more time on LLCs, because these seem to be very popular right now and most of my clients come to my office wanting to set up this type of entity.

Single-Member or Multi-Member

In an LLC, the owners are called members. An LLC can have only one member, or it can have multiple members. Each member may have the same rights in the LLC, or different rights. For example, some members may have voting rights while others may just have a right to receive equity in the business without the right to vote or make major decisions that will affect the business. The members can also be the managers, managing the day-to-day operations of the business (though they don't have to be).

The first step will be creating an Operating Agreement. This will lay out the rights and responsibilities of the members. In creating your Operating Agreement, you will need to decide what rights you want to give the members. Will they all be equal? Will all members have voting rights on the business or will some members have a right to equity, but should not vote on the operations? Will the profits and losses all be equal, or will some have bigger and smaller percentages of profits and loss?

Let's go back to your friend's cookie shop. In this scenario, let's say you both decide to go into it together but she is going to run the day-to-day operations. You may decide you will both be voting members and she will be the manager. Maybe you will actually have more of a voting interest because you put in more money. Conversely, maybe because she put in "sweat equity, "you both have equal voting rights (sweat equity, remember, means that she is not actually putting in *money*, but rather her hard work and knowledge). LLCs can be very flexible and are widely popular for these reasons.

When determining if an LLC is a good fit for you, you may want to consider how many owners you eventually want to have. If it's a larger number, say around or over 35, you may want to consider a corporation rather than an LLC. LLCs are a really good option for *small* businesses. They are easier to run with fewer owners and allow for flexibility in doing so. However, if you need 35 members to vote on a new direction, that could be more difficult.

Side note: not everyone is allowed to create an LLC. For example, in California, here is a list of professions that cannot form an LLC:

- accountants
- lawyers
- architects
- chiropractors
- clinical social workers
- court reporters
- dentists
- doctors
- marriage counselors
- nurses, optometrists
- pharmacists
- physical therapists
- psychologists
- veterinarians

Whether or not your profession can form an LLC will depend on your state, and a lawyer in your state will be able to tell you if an LLC is appropriate for you.

If you do decide to create an LLC, you will need to file the Articles of Organization with the state. You will also need to obtain an EIN for the entity. You may also wish to create an Operating Agreement, which states the terms of the LLC. This would be similar to the Partnership Agreement mentioned above, but for an LLC. It will lay out who does and gets what from the business.

Taxes

LLCs give a variety of ways to be taxed. They can be taxed as a pass-through entity (as stated above), as a partnership, as a disregarded entity, or as an S Corp or C Corp. Your tax treatment will coincide with the purpose and intent of the LLC. Ask your accountant and/or attorney which one is right for you.

Rental Properties

I have a lot of clients who like the idea of owning a rental property. Many of my clients do this and make a decent amount from it. Let's create a hypothetical wherein you buy that awesome vacation home you plan to rent out during the year. Buying the house was easy to do, you listed it on a couple of websites, and *voila,* your place is a hot spot. Over the summer, you generate a decent percent of passive income.[13] You did not, however, seek out an attorney for recommendations to make sure you were protected. In fact, you didn't even know that what you were doing could be considered a "business." I'm here to tell you that it can and should be run as a business, so when that bachelorette party gets a little too wild and one falls through the porch board, your personal checking and savings accounts are not on the line.

---

[13] Passive income – income you do not have work for, but comes to you even when you are not working on or in the business.

When purchasing many different rental properties, sometimes clients like to set up what is called a "Series LLC." A series creates the parent company and then has a subsidiary created for each individual rental property. In this scenario, the biggest attraction is how the liability for each series is limited to its individual series and does not take on the risk and liability of the other rental units.

Series LLC's are not allowed in every state—but it is growing in popularity. If you own multiple businesses for the same purpose, you may want to look into whether this is an option for you there, as well.

Managing Your Business

If you create an LLC but don't manage it properly, it is *not likely* to protect you! The next big crucial step after creating an LLC is to make sure you run your LLC (or any other business) as the separate entity that it is—meaning, apart from your personal accounts. This means creating a business bank account and accepting the rent checks to your business name, not you personally. It also means making sure any repairs and expenses come out of the business accounts, not personal accounts. Doing small things like this shows that you are doing things on the up and up. You intended to create a business, you went through the process to draft all the documents and file correctly, and now you are managing it like one. This can all be evidence to the court to show *why* the court should not "pierce the corporate veil" and allow access to your personal assets.

Connecting the Dots

The fascinating thing about the legal world is that it all connects together—and because of that, you will want to incorporate your interest in your business into your estate plan. With an LLC, usually all the members have a right to vote on assignments of interest. However, some Operating Agreements will have a clause stating that a member is allowed to transfer his or her interest into their trust or through their wills. Even if the Operating Agreement does not have a clause like this, it will usually have some statement on what happens upon the passing of one member. This is not only important for the estate, but also the remaining members. The other members should carefully consider how the interest of a deceased member will be paid for. Maybe there will be enough cash in the business to pay off the estate, or maybe it will be paid out over five years.

Another option is to purchase a life insurance policy to cover the member's interests. This will help the other members in the event that one member passes, so they don't have to suddenly cough up a ton of dough. Also, if that member was also a manager and actually working in the business, you may want to consider taking out a policy big enough to cover the expenses to pay someone to do that job.

Business Tip

Consider insurance to protect your business. This can be a general liability insurance, in case someone slips and falls in the building. You may also want to consider disability insurance. When you work for a company, this is usually provided, with the company either offering short-and/or long-term disability insurance. This ensures that if you become disabled and are no longer able to work, you will have enough to provide for your basic needs. When you are out in your own cookie shop, you are the boss, and that means you should provide for this type of protection! This can be huge help if you get into a car accident and need to pay your bills. It can also help cover the overhead expenses of the company while you are in the transition period of hiring people to take over your role.

Tip of the Iceberg

Once you start your business, there will be a whole host of other issues you will encounter and need to consider. For example, having a company handbook, employment agreements, rental agreements, etc. The aforementioned are just the very first decisions you will need to decide and do in order to create your business. They are not exhaustive, and are merely meant to help you start thinking of what you want your business to look like.

Big-Ass Disclaimer

One of my favorite quotes ever is, "the only thing constant in life is change." Like the rest of the world is always changing, so are laws. The laws may have changed from the time I wrote this book to the time you are reading it. Likewise, the structures or tax implications for the various entities I mention here may have changed, too. To ensure the best entity for you, go see a local attorney. To ensure you are creating the one that will have the best tax advantage for you, go see your local accountant. *Please do this!* It will be well worth the money spent.

Summary

To summarize, if you're going to start a business, consider the type of formal entity that is a right fit for you. That may be an S-Corp, a general partnership, or an LLC. How you set it up will determine the distributions, the taxes, and the liability, so you may want to meet with your attorney and accountant to discuss beforehand.

PART V
EXTRAS

Here are some extra tidbits of information and things
to consider when looking for an attorney.

THE BIG BAD WOLF

I want to give you some advice that applies to the legal industry, as well as to other industries. I have paid particular attention to this because: 1) I am a lawyer (obviously), and 2) I am a small business owner.

There are many industries out there that are being crippled by big corporations. These corporations are allowed to come in and own a business, even though the owners are not licensed, do not practice in the area, and do not have any real idea of what it takes to be good at the particular trade. They may not even give two cares about the industry!

Why is this bad?

Well, most business owners' bottom line is profit. In order to maximize profit, they need to figure out how to make the "widget" they are selling or the service they are providing cheaper, so they can drive up profit. When big businesses enter into a profession they do not practice in, they can accomplish cheaper service by hiring novice-level employees and paying them less. Even if the professional they hire is not a novice and is actually really great in their trade, they will most likely pay them less than what that person would make if these big bad wolves did not come in and overrun the trade.

The result?

Overworked employees working for less money, which equals…wait for it… poorer-quality service and products!

This is nothing new. Growing up, my grandparents told me the story of how they owned and ran three local bakeries in Chicago, Illinois. Once superstores started taking over the world, they put all the little neighborhood bakeries completely out of business. That included my grandfather's three bakeries where he, his wife, and his three children all worked. It not only hurt the small businesses, but also the product. My grandparents made the best kolaches,[14] and the world is now sadly missing out on them.

What is new though, and why I am mentioning this in this book, is that this concept has moved into professional industries.

Legislation has started to sweep across the nation to allow big business to take over professional industries, like lawyers and doctors' offices. You may feel that lawyers and doctors make enough money, and that they can cry you a river about the corporate giants taking over, but, remember that *service* thing I mentioned? You may not care now, but you will care when it comes to the doctor potentially saving your life by actually giving a hoot about their job.

On that same note, this is why many people prefer to opt into a Preferred Provider Organization (PPO) instead of a Health Maintenance Organization (HMO). Although you may pay more for a doctor's services in a PPO, when you are hiring a professional, you generally want the one that is going to do the best work, not the one that is the least expensive.

This is all very close to home to me, as I have a lot of moles on my body and fortunately learned about the importance of getting them checked through clients of mine. I learned just how scary and deadly melanoma can be, so, I looked up my "local dermatology center" and scheduled an appointment. It was an open, beautiful, and bright office that was impressive upon walking in. I thought, wow, from the appearance, I must really be in a good place of business and felt like I could trust them. I felt like I was walking into a spa instead of an old drab doctor's office.

I got scanned for skin cancer and they found a few suspicious moles. They performed surgery on me in numerous places on my body. Each time I went, I had a different doctor. Even though they took notes for the next doctor to review, I didn't have a specialist who actually knew my name. I had been there many times, and none of the nurses or doctors even knew

---

[14] A delicious Polish cookie.

who I was. They didn't know me or my body from Adam. They couldn't tell you that I have two little boys and how important it is to me to be very conservative when scanning or doing biopsies. They couldn't tell you that through my estate planning practice, I had dealt with too many young widows and widowers with young children who had recently lost their spouses to melanoma.

Needless to say, after a couple years with the awful feeling of just being a number to them, I decided to finally try a different dermatologist's office. This time, the doctor's name was in the practice name, so I knew I was meeting with someone who cared enough to link their reputation to their business. I'm so glad I went to see this new dermatologist, as she immediately found a suspicious mole. She said it was not the type of mole that "screamed" melanoma, but she had a bad feeling about it. Since she actually knew my story (that I have two young sons and wanted her to test anything that was suspicious), we did. Guess what? It turned out to be in the beginning stages of melanoma. I'm forever grateful to my awesome dermatologist (who also has a very cute office by the way) and so glad I left the big corporate dermatologists. Since then, my doctor has found other moles that were in the beginning stages of melanoma and I have been lucky enough to catch them. I'm repeatedly grateful that I trusted my gut and left the first office to find a doctor that knows my name.

The wolves in sheep's clothing are not just linked to dermatologists. Be careful, and do research before you hire a seemingly corporate doctor, accountant, financial advisor, or other *professional*.

A word to the wise: before you hire a big retain chain cloaked in a certain profession's attire, do some research and see what the qualifications are to work there. A bachelor's degree in accounting (at the big tax preparer), or simply a high school diploma? Ask the person helping you how much training they had. If it was simply a few weeks of training with a high school diploma, you may want to consider taking your money elsewhere. However, if only getting the minimum is what's important to you and/or that is what you can afford, then by all means, go to the place that offers inexpensive professional services.

As you may have guessed, this approach is a growing trend in the legal industry, as well. This allows people who are not lawyers to come in and own law firms, and tell lawyers how they should conduct their professional services. This will likely drive down costs, which is great for the client but will just put pressure to serve more people and give mediocre service.

Again, you may hate lawyers and don't care. The thing is, everyone hates lawyers… until they need one! When you actually *need* a lawyer, are you going to want the one that is forced to have an overload of cases? I think we've all heard of the horror stories of the overworked public defenders.

It just drives home the point: if the subject matter is really important to you, you may want to find an attorney who is going to be dedicated to your matter.

Okay, back to the point. If you want specialized service, I suggest seeking out your local professionals and paying for it. It will be worth it. If you want to get the most money back on your income tax returns, or if you want the doctor who is going to know your body, or if you want the lawyer who is going to actually help your family when your mom passes, then you may want to look for an actual professional. You know, like one who went to school to learn the trade, knows your name, and your file. In this day and age, what you don't know can and will hurt you. Many large corporations take advantage of the fact that just looking like a sheep is enough to trick many people.

Luckily, we are starting to see a rise of specialized small businesses again, as people have learned that lower prices and lower quality are not always the most desirable option. There are services and products out there that are *worth* paying more for, and I would argue that legal services are one of them.

In conclusion, when choosing the law firm (or any business that you're working with, really), make sure to do your due diligence, they are qualified, and a good fit for what you need.

CLOSING TIME

W e've gone through a lot of legal stuff, so here is a recap.
If you need an attorney and not sure where to go, or heard horror stories from friends with bad experiences, don't worry! There are many resources out there and new ways legal services are delivered and billed now. You may want to consult with your specific state or county's bar association to see if they have any referrals for you. You can also feel free to reach out to Campbell Long, LLC. Even if you do not fall within our geographic or practice area, we can try to find a referral for you!

Generally, when life is changing, it's usually a good idea to talk with an attorney. Of course, there are other times, that are a little more obvious, when an attorney is needed, such as in dealing with criminal issues. But there are other times that are not as obvious.

Attorneys can help with everything from getting your wills in place to assisting with the purchase of your home, and everything in between. Here is a list of some of the most popular times to reach out for legal advice:

- Setting up estate planning documents (wills, trusts, and powers of attorney)
- Obtaining a Guardianship (or Conservatorship) over another
- Probating a deceased's estate
- Divorce
- Premarital and Post Marital Agreements
- Buying or Selling Real Estate
- Adopting a Child
- Creating a Business

So don't be afraid to reach out to your attorney and ask if they have recommendations for your current situation. Personally, I love when my prior clients call or email me to discuss what's going on in their life and checking in to see if there is anything they should be doing. Sometimes I can help them, sometimes I can't and refer them to an attorney who can, and sometimes legal services are not needed. But I love that they feel knowledgeable and comfortable enough to reach out to ask. This makes it easier in the long run to help protect them from unwanted situations.

Well, that's all folks. I hope this book helps you avoid or get out of sticky legal situations. And if nothing else, I hope it gives you the information to know when you should see an attorney, and ideas of what to ask about when you do.

Made in the USA
Middletown, DE
12 March 2022